Abdelaziz OUADAH

Skyline-based models for Web Services Selection

Abdelaziz OUADAH

Skyline-based models for Web Services Selection

Skyline Models and Algorithms for Web Services Selection Based on Invocation History

ScienciaScripts

Imprint

Cover image: www.ingimage.com

This book is a translation from the original published under ISBN 978-620-6-72382-0.

Publisher:
Sciencia Scripts
is a trademark of
Dodo Books Indian Ocean Ltd. and OmniScriptum S.R.L publishing group

120 High Road, East Finchley, London, N2 9ED, United Kingdom
Str. Armeneasca 28/1, office 1, Chisinau MD-2012, Republic of Moldova, Europe
Printed at: see last page
ISBN: 978-620-8-34057-5

Contents

Dedication

I dëdie this modest work:

In memory of my mother and my father, may Allah accept them into his vast paradise,

Resume

With the proliferation of service-orientedë architectures in recent years, the number of services published on the Web has increased exponentially. To select a service from a number of candidate services, which offer the same functionality but with different quality of services (QoS), 1 user cannot test all the candidate services, instead they can base their selection on the history of previous invocations made by other users. In recent years, Skyline has emerged as a popular new paradigm for finding the most relevant Web services based on QoS data. It is a promising approach that reduces the user's decision space by offering only those services that are not dominated; however, Skyline has some drawbacks: i) it returns incomparable results, ii) it gives the same importance to all QoS criteria, iii) the Skyline result size cannot be controlled.

In this paper, we discuss several proposals to address these issues: the first, called SkyAP-S3, is based on the combination of several multicriteria decision support methods (MCDMs), namely: Skyline to reduce the search space, AHP to weight QoS criteria, PROMETHEE to capture user preferences and rank Skyline Web services. The second proposal, called SEFAP, is an improved version of SkyAP-S3, and involves dealing with uncertainty in user judgements when weighting QoS criteria. We have used the objective data-based method "Entropy" and the subjective user judgement-based method "Fuzzy AHP".

In the third approach, we propose an improved version of the Fuzzy AHP method for ranking Skyline Web services, such that comparison matrices between QoS criteria and between representative Skyline Web services will be generated automatically by exploiting a discretisation algorithm on QoS data.

To demonstrate the effectiveness of our approaches, experiments were carried out and comparative studies with existing approaches were also discussed.

Keywords : Skyline, Web services, AHP, AHP Floue, PROMETHEE, Quality of service, user preferences.

General introduction

1.1 Context

In recent years, modern businesses have had to respond very effectively to the opportunities offered by an increasingly competitive and complex market. To do this, they face a number of requirements in terms of the interoperability, maintenance and integration of their business applications, both inside and outside the company. These requirements have increased the need for a modern architecture based on recognised standards. Service Oriented Architecture (SOA) represents the platform most adopted by enterprises to meet the needs of business applications in terms of low coupling, standardisation and platform independence in order to automate the business process [Papazoglou el al., 2007].

According to [MacKenzie et al. 2006], SOA is an abstract framework for understanding the meanings of the entities that make it up and the relationships between these entities. [Papazoglou 2003] defines SOA as a paradigm that uses Web services as fundamental elements for application development, a way of reorganising infrastructures and software solutions into a set of interactive services. Another definition given by [Arsanjani 2004], SOA is a concept based on an architectural style that defines a mode of interaction between three main parties: the provider, the directory and the consumer. The service provider creates and describes the services, the directory publishes the services and makes them accessible to users and applications, the consumer explores and discovers the services, selects the relevant services that can satisfy their needs and invokes them through standard interfaces and protocols. According to [Erl 2004], one of the objectives of SOA is to provide added value to the solution implemented, using modern approaches to the analysis, design and development of applications.

Web services are software components that represent the basic elements of SOA, they can be published and invoked on the Web using a set of standards such as SOAP to structure exchange messages between software components, WSDL to describe the Operations offered by each service and how to interact with it, UDDI to publish and locate services on the Web [Curbera et al., 2002].

Each service is contiguous in order to perform a specific task. A service is described by its identifier on the Web and its input and output parameters, which represent its functional information. However, there is other non-functional information that can characterise the Web service, such as response time, availability, price of the service, reliability, etc. This information is called Quality of Service (QoS). Quality of Service has become a crucial criterion in the process of selecting and composing Web services offered by different suppliers with similar functionalities.

1.2 Problems

The quality of service obtained from service descriptors (WSDL) or service providers (UDDI) does not reflect the real quality of these services. It differs from one user to another, from one context to another, and changes dynamically over time as a function of several parameters [Yu et al., 2009]. For example, the execution time of a Web service can vary depending on network traffic and the ability of the service itself to maintain the same performance (scalability) with a significant increase in the number of simultaneous invocations.

According to statistics published by the Web services directory Programmable Web[1] , and by

[1] https://www.programmableWeb.com/

the Web services search engine *services.Seekda.com*, the number of services published on the Web in recent years has increased exponentially [He et al., 2017], and the use of these services by users has generated a large amount of data on invocation history [Zhang et al., 2018]. However, to select a service from several candidate services, which offer the same functionality but with different service qualities, the user cannot test all the candidate services, but can rely on the history of previous invocations made by other users in similar contexts [Shao et al., 2007]. Exploiting the experience of other users provides information about the real quality of these services, and then helps the user to choose the best services.

In recent years, the notion of Skyline [Borzsonyi et al., 2001] has emerged as a new and popular paradigm for finding the most relevant Web services. This is a promising direction to reduce the user's decision space by offering only the most intëressant services, and consequently simplify the sëlection process. However, Skyline has come in for some criticism:

1) The size of the Skyline result cannot be controlled. In fact, the Skyline result can be large and demanding, requiring a great deal of effort to process, or it can be very small and inconsistent for the user;

2) Skyline generally returns conflicting and incomparable results, which makes the selection process very difficult for the user;

3) Skyline places the same importance on selection criteria (QoS), however, the importance of QoS differs from one context to another and from one user to another, for example, in the context of e-payment, the security criterion is more important than the other criteria, but in the context of information retrieval, response time is the most important criterion.

To remedy the first drawback, and to allow the user to control the size of the Skyline result, the K-representative Skyline variant was proposed [Lin et al., 2007] [Tao et al., 2009], which returns a subset of the Skyline result that represents the total Skyline result. Nevertheless, this variant returns an incomparable result, where the user finds it difficult to choose the best services that meet their preferences.

Several approaches proposed in the literature have exploited Multi-Criteria Decision Making (MCDM) methods for the treatment of incomparability between alternatives and the selection of Web services, such as Analytic Hierarchy Process (AHP) and PROMETEE. However, these methods generally deal with datasets where the number of services is very limited. Nevertheless, the number of services offering the same functionalities with different service qualities is increasing daily, which makes the use of these approaches very difficult, particularly in the context of Web service selection.

The AHP method [Saaty 1987] is widely used for weighting criteria and ranking alternatives. It has the advantage of modelling the hierarchical fagon problem, and weighing the selection criteria based on the comparison between each two criteria using the Saaty scale [Saaty 1987], expressed in linguistic form. However, this method has some drawbacks, in particular: the subjectivity and imprecision of users' opinions when filling several comparison matrices between criteria and between alternatives for ranking the latter. This opëraňoп requires a lot of effort for 1 user. Also, if the cohërence test fails, the user has to redo all the work of reconstructing these comparison matrices (the cohërence index IC dëpasse 0.1).

1.3 Contributions

The main contributions of this thesis are rësumëes in the proposal of three approaches for the sëlection of Skyline Web services:

- **SkyAP-S3 approach: Combining Skyline with AHP and PROMETHEE**

To overcome the inconvënients prësentës by the Skyline mëthod in terms of result incomparability and the weightëration of QoS criteria, we propose an approach based on the combination of the Skyline opërateur with the multicriteria dëcision support methods AHP and PROMETHEE [Ouadah et al., 2015a] [Ouadah et al., 2015b]. The Skyline opërator is usedë to reduce the search space by focusing only on relevant services that are not domiiK'd by any other service, domiiK'd services are ëcartës automatically from the sëlection process. This first ëtape is performed offline and the Skyline result is recalculated after each QoS donees update or after the insertion of a new Web service. The AHP (Analytic Hierarchy Process) method is used to weight QoS criteria in a simple and intuitive way, relying on linguistic terms for comparison between QoS criteria and allowing the user's judgements to be checked for consistency. The PROMETHEE method is explored for the ranking of Skyline Web services thanks to the over-ranking relationships between Web services, ultimately providing the user with a ranked list of Skyline Web services that most closely match their prëfërences.

- **SEFAP approach: Objective and subjective weighting of QoS criteria**

Although the AHP method is frequently used for criterion weighting, it is criticised for its inability to deal with the imprecision of user judgements. Indeed, prëfërences are expressed in numeric form ^ Saaty scale [Saaty 1987]). In this approach we focus on the treatment of subjectivity and imprecision in the process of weightëration of QoS criteria, we adapt the SkyAP-S3 approach, replacing the AHP mëthod by both Shannon Entropy and Fuzzy AHP mëthods [Ouadah et al., 2018a]. The Entropy mëthod extracts objective weights of QoS criteria from invocation history data by exploiting QoS data. Whereas, Fuzzy AHP exploits the subjective opinion of the user and triangular fuzzy numbers for gbnbration of comparison matrices between criteria.

- **IFAHP approach: an improved version of fuzzy AHP for the selection of representative Web services**

This approach is divided into two steps: to control the size of the result returned by the Skyline operator, we adopt a variant of the Skyline operator called "K- reprbsentative Skyline" [Ouadah et al., 2018b] [Ouadah et al, 2018c], the latter makes it possible to return a representative summary of the Skyline result, this will make it possible to reduce the size and return an exploitable sample by the user, and as the K-reprbsentative Skyline variant returns a set of conflicting and incomparable services, we propose an ambliorbe version of the Fuzzy AHP method [Ouadah et al, 2018d], this version allows on the one hand to blicit the importance of QoS criteria using linguistic terms based on a natural language. On the other hand, it considerably reduces the number of comparisons and automatically generates comparison matrices between alternatives for each QoS criterion, based on a discrtisation algorithm transforming quantitative data into qualitative data, and numerical attributes into discrete attributes with a finite number of intervals.

1.4 Organisation of these

Our thesis manuscript is structured in two parts: the first part presents our state of the art, which is structured around three chapters and encompasses three research areas. The second part, entitled "Contributions", describes the three approaches proposed for the selection of Skyline Web services and the experiments carried out to validate these approaches.

Part I "State of the Art" consists of three chapters:

- **Chapter 2: Web services**

In this chapter, we first present some definitions of the Web service concept, then we describe the Web services model and its components, and then we mention the Web services standards: WSDL, the service description language, SOAP, the service transport protocol, and UDDI, the service publication directory. Finally, we present examples of directories for publishing UDDI services on the Web.

- **Chapter 3: Selecting Skyline Web Services**

In this chapter, we define the notion of Skyline, we then present the algorithms as well as some variants of Skyline, we will cite afterwards, some examples of research works that use Skyline algorithms for the sëlection of Web services. At the end of this chapter, we will present a comparative study between these works based on a certain number of criteria.

- **Chapter 4: Web services selection based on MCDM methods**

This chapter is devoted to the presentation of multicriteria dëcision support methods and their classifications as well as existing approaches that use MCDM mëthods for Web services sëlection. At the end of this chapter, we will present a ëcomparative study between these approaches.

Part II "Contribution" comprises two chapters:

- **Chapter 5: Proposed approaches**

In this chapter we describe the three approaches proposed in our thesis, namely :

o SkyAP approach: for the selection of Web services, in order to reduce the search space and offer the user a ranked list of Web services that best meet their preferences.

o SEFAP approach: to exploit the MCDM Entropy and Fuzzy AHP methods for the objective and subjective weighting of QoS criteria,

o IFAHP approach: for the selection of K-representative Skyline Web services, which controls the size of the Skyline result and returns a representative summary of the entire Skyline result; a new version of the Fuzzy AHP method has been proposed for tidying up the selected services with minimum effort on the part of the user.

- **Chapter 6: Implementation and Experimentation**

This final chapter is devoted to the implementation and validation of the proposed approaches. A series of experiments have been carried out to demonstrate the feasibility and effectiveness of these approaches, based on real data sets.

We end our report with a general conclusion and a few thoughts on the future.

Part I

State of the art

2 Web Services

2.1 Introduction

One of the aims of Service Oriented Architectures (SOA) is to enable a low level of coupling between the Web services that make up a system. The clients of these services do not need to know details about their technical implementations or the platforms on which they have been deployed. This facilitates interoperability between platforms and enables several Web services from different sources to be integrated into a single application. Using the functionality offered by existing Web services reduces application development time and complexity. However, when selecting a Web service to integrate into an application, it is important to choose the best Web services that offer similar functionality but with different QoS.

In this chapter, we first present some definitions of the notion of Web service, then we describe the Web services model and its elements, and then we present the Web services standards: WSDL the service description language, SOAP the service transport protocol, RESTful the HTTP-based Web services style and UDDI the service publication directory. Finally, we will present examples of Web service publication directories.

2.2 Definition

In the literature there are several definitions for a Web service, the definition given by the dictionary: "*a service is an action performed by one entity for another*" [Marin 2008]. It is therefore necessary to know the details of this action before using it.

A Web service is defined by [Papazoglou et al., 2003] as being "*a software entity that can be used through its description*". Using a service does not require knowledge of the technologies used to implement it, or the platform on which it runs. In the same way, a Web service does not impose any constraints in terms of implementation and deployment technologies on the user who consumes it in his program. This independence in both directions is a major advantage, enabling a single application to use several Web services developed using different technologies and deployed on different platforms.

A software service is "*a piece of software that is made available to other applications. For a service to be usable, it must be described, published and its capabilities known by its users*" [Marin 2008].

[Gottschalk 2000] gives the following definition of Web services: "*Web services are self-contained and self-describing that can be published, located and invoked over the Web, using a set of standards such as SOAP (Simple Object Access Protocol), WSDL (Web Service Description Language) and UDDI (Universal Description Discovery and Integration)*".

The W3C consortium [Booth et al., 2004] defines a service as "*an application or software component identified by a URI (Uniform Resource Identifier), whose interfaces and links are described in XML (eXtensible Markup Language). Its description can be discovered by other Web services, and it can interact with other Web services using standard Internet protocols*".

From the client's point of view, the Web service is a "black box" that does not give any details about its implementation. The Web service receives a request from a client, processes this request and finally sends its response to the client [Marin 2008].

Web services support two styles of communication: synchronous and asynchronous [Papazoglou el al 2004]. For the synchronous type, Web service clients send their requests as a call to a mëthod with a set of paraтëйез inputs and wait for the response before continuing their exëcutions. This type of communication requires a strong coupling between the client

and the service, as the client always remains waiting for a response from the service. In asynchronous communication, the client and service exchange messages. The client sends a message to the service and continues its exëcution without waiting for the reply, and in this way the client is less strongly coupled to the invoked service. The service processes the request and can respond instantly or postpone the response.
"*Web services are described in a formal way by the names and types of input and output parameters and constraints*" [Benouaret 2012a]. The input/output paramëtres represent its functional information, while the other non-functional information such as response time, availability, price, are the quality of services (QoS).
We can say that a Web service is a software component that offers a well-defined functionality, it can be used by clients or by other services by relying on Internet standards for its description, its invocation and its interactions. The behaviour of a service is described by functional information such as its inputs and outputs.

2.3 Web services players and operations

Web services technology [Papazoglou el al., 2004] is based on the interaction between three types of participants. Three operations are used: service publication, service search or discovery and service binding or invocation.

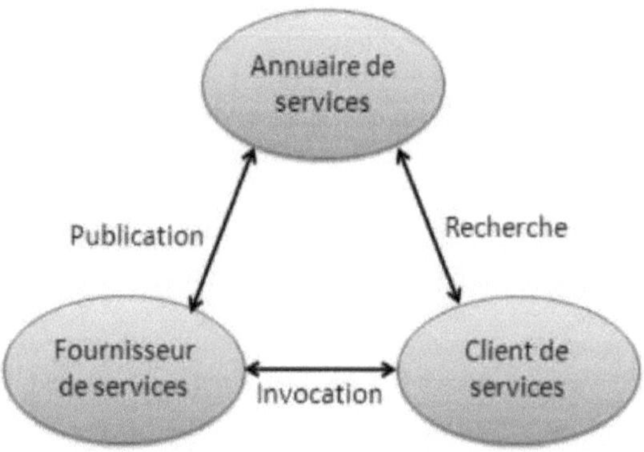

Figure 1. Web services actors and operations [Papazoglou el al., 2004].
The three main elements of the Web service model are :

- **The service provider**: the service provider implements the service, deploys the service on a deployment platform, publishes the service on a directory and describes the service to give customers all the information about the service.
- **The service directory**: provides service providers with the resources they need to publish their services and the means for customers to search and discover them.
- **The service client**: the client searches for the desired Web service in a directory, usually by keyword. The client selects the service and uses the description information to invoke the service.

The interactions between these three elements are described as follows:
o **Publication**: publication of the service enables other users to find it. It consists of firstly writing the Web service and secondly registering it in a directory to make it accessible to

clients.

o **Search**: searching for a Web service involves first discovering it in the service directory, then choosing the service to be searched for from among several found. Two sëlection methods are possible: manual and automatic. In manual sëlection, the user chooses the service directly, while for automatic sëlection, a special client application (Broker) can perform this task.

o **Invocation**: this is Гopëration most important, during this opëration the service requester invokes or exëcutes in real time the service using details provided by the service descriptor. Two types of invocation are possible: the first type is a direct invocation through the information provided by the service descriptor and the second type is an invocation through an intermëdiary (Broker).

2.4 Web services standards

2.4.1 WSDL (Web Services Description Language)

The need for a clear description of the communication between clients and services has led to the standardisation of this description using well-structured XML files. WSDL is a standard used to normalise the description of Web services. In the following section, we present the WSDL service description language, the structure of the WSDL file, the ëlë elements making up the file and its various versions [Lopez-Velasco 2008].

The first work to emerge concerning the Web Service Description Language (WSDL) was the W3C work in 2001 [Christensen et al., 2001]. The aim ëTяH to propose a language that is interpretable and comprehensible by a large number of platforms. This description includes the methods and parameters of Web services that can be invoked via SOAP messages. The different elements described in a WSDL file are :

- Operations offered by the Web service
- The donees and messages ëchangës during the service call
- The communications protocol
- The service access port

2.4.2 SOAP (Simple Object Access Protocol)

SOAP is the protocol usedë for the exchange of messages between the client and the Web service, relying on the XML language as ëbeing a standard format for exchanging structured data, mdëpendently of development platforms, programming languages or operating systëmes. SOAP can be ийНзë in any style of synchronous or asynchronous communication [Box et al., 2000].

SOAP is mainly based on the HTTP and XML standards [Ben Halima 2009] :

S HTTP as ëbeing a SOAP message transport protocol. It is a good means of transport thanks to its popularity^ on the Web.

S XML as ëtant un langage standard d'echange de données semi-structurees, concernant les requetes, les réponses aux requetes, les paramëtres d'entrees et de sorties, ...ect.

The structure of a SOAP message is given in [Mitra et al,. 2007], and consists of two parts, the transport protocol header and the SOAP envelope.

2.4.2.1 The transport protocol header :

It depends on the protocol used, such as HTTP. If HTTP is used, the header will have the following content:

✓ The http protocol version

✓ The date of gënëration of the SOAP message.

✓ The type of content encoding.
✓ The name and version of the application server
✓ Implementation technology

```
HTTP/1.1 200 OK
Cache-Control: private, max-age=0
Content-Type: text/xml; charset=utf-8
Vary: Accept-Encoding
Server: Microsoft-IIS/7.0
X-AspNet-Version: 4.0.30319
X-Powered-By: ASP.NET
Date: Mon, 06 Jan 2014 10:19:22 GMT
Content-Length: 687
Proxy-Connection: Keep-Alive
Connection: Keep-Alive
Content-Encoding: gzip
```

.etc.

Figure 2. Example of a transport protocol header.

2.4.2.2 SOAP envelope :

It represents the main part of the SOAP message and is made up of two parts, the header and the body.

- SOAP message header :

It is an optional element, a flexible mechanism for extending the message or adding information in a dĕcentralisedĕe and modular way. Typical examples of extensions that can be implemented as input to the SOAP message header: authentication, transaction management, etc.

The tags delimiting this part are <SOAP-ENV :Header> and </SOAP- ENV :Header>.

The four main attributes that make up the en-tete part are [Gudgin et al 2003]:

✓ *EncodingStyle* : indicates the encoding rules used to serialise the various parts of the SOAP message, transforming them into an XML stream.

✓ *Role*: indicates the SOAP node to which the SOAP block en-tete is destined.

✓ *mustUnderstand :* indicates whether processing of the SOAP header block is mandatory or optional.

✓ *relay*: indicates whether the regu message should be redirected to another nceud if it has not been processed.

```
<SOAP-ENV:Header>
<t:Transaction xmlns:t="some-URI" SOAP-ENV:mustUnderstand="1">
5
</t:Transaction>
</SOAP-ENV:Header>
```

Figure 3. Example of a SOAP message header.

In this example, the SOAP envelope header carries additional information about the identifier of the transaction being processed, via *the <Transaction>* tag. The value of the *mustUnderstand= 1* attribute, indicates that processing of the header is mandatory.

- Message body SOAP

The body of the SOAP message provides a simple mechanism for exchanging information between the client and the service. The tags that delimit this part are <soap :Body> and </soap :Body>.

The following two figures show an example of a SOAP invocation and response message for the GlobalWeather Web service described in its WSDL file (http ://www.Webservicex.com/globalweather.asmx?wsdl). This is a service offered by the Web services provider *WebserviceX.net*. This service accepts as input the city and country (example: Bejaia and Algeria), and returns as response a set of information about the mëtëorology ^етрёraIIIre, wind speed, visibilitë, mëtëorological conditions, ...).

```xml
<soap:Envelope xmlns:soap="http://www.w3.org/2003/05/soap-envelope" xmlns:web="http://www.webserviceX.NET">
   <soap:Header/>
   <soap:Body>
      <web:GetWeather>
         <!--Optional:-->
         <web:CityName>Bejaia</web:CityName>
         <!--Optional:-->
         <web:CountryName>Algeria</web:CountryName>
      </web:GetWeather>
   </soap:Body>
</soap:Envelope>
```

Figure 4: Example of a SOAP request message.

```xml
<soap:Envelope xmlns:soap="http://www.w3.org/2003/05/soap-envelope" xmlns:xsi="http://www.w3.org/2001/XMLSchem
   <soap:Body>
      <GetWeatherResponse xmlns="http://www.webserviceX.NET">
         <GetWeatherResult><![CDATA[<?xml version="1.0" encoding="utf-16"?>
<CurrentWeather>
  <Location>Bejaia, Algeria (DAAE) 36-43N 005-04E 2M</Location>
  <Time>Dec 31, 2013 - 04:00 AM EST / 2013.12.31 0900 UTC</Time>
  <Wind> from the W (280 degrees) at 16 MPH (14 KT):0</Wind>
  <Visibility> greater than 7 mile(s):0</Visibility>
  <SkyConditions> mostly clear</SkyConditions>
  <Temperature> 48 F (9 C)</Temperature>
  <DewPoint> 42 F (6 C)</DewPoint>
  <RelativeHumidity> 81%</RelativeHumidity>
  <Pressure> 30.30 in. Hg (1026 hPa)</Pressure>
  <Status>Success</Status>
</CurrentWeather>]]></GetWeatherResult>
      </GetWeatherResponse>
   </soap:Body>
</soap:Envelope>
```

Figure 5: Example of a SOAP response message.

2.4.3 RESTful (REepresentational State Transfer)

RESTful is a Web services architecture developed by Roy Fielding in his thesis in 2000 [Fielding et al., 2000]. This architecture is based on the use of Web standards developed by W3C: HTTP, URL and XML. RESTful allows Web services to be invoked in a uniform manner by exploiting HTTP protocol methods: GET, POST, PUT, and DELETE.

2.4.4 UDDI (Universal Description Discovery and Integration)

UDDI is a specification that provides users with a unified and systematic way of finding service providers through a centralized service registry [Curbera et al., 2002]. UDDI provides two basic specifications that define the structure of the registry:

1. Definition of the information to be provided for each service.
2. Definition of the APIs available for accessing and updating this information.

Access to the registry is achieved using the SOAP standard for access and update.

2.4.4.1 UDDI directories on the Web

There are UDDI directories on the Web. The purpose of these directories is to publish Web services offered by suppliers and make them accessible. On the other hand, to facilitate the search, discovery and use of these services. In the following, we will describe two examples of UDDI directories: Xmethods[2] , remoteMethods[3] [Lopez velasco 2008]

2.4.4.1.1 Xmethods

Xmethods is a directory for publishing, searching and accessing Web services. This directory contains no fewer than 400 Web services.

To publish a service, the provider must be registered on the Xmethods site[1] , and must provide all the information required to create a new entry in the directory, such as the name of the service, the WSDL description, the location of the service, etc., while complying with the

[2] http://xmethods.com, last accessed January 2017.
[3] http://www.remotemethods.com, last access January 2017[4] http://xmethods.com, last access January 2017.

UDDI spëcifications. In addition the provider must provide other information requested by Xmethods[1] such as email.
The Xmethods directory[1] displays public Web services in the form of a list. This list contains the following information: the service provider (Publisher), the style (RPC, DOC, .), the service name, the service description, the implementation type (.NET, AXIS, .etc.) and a test link. However, the user can access detailed information about the Web service, such as the content of the WSDL document.

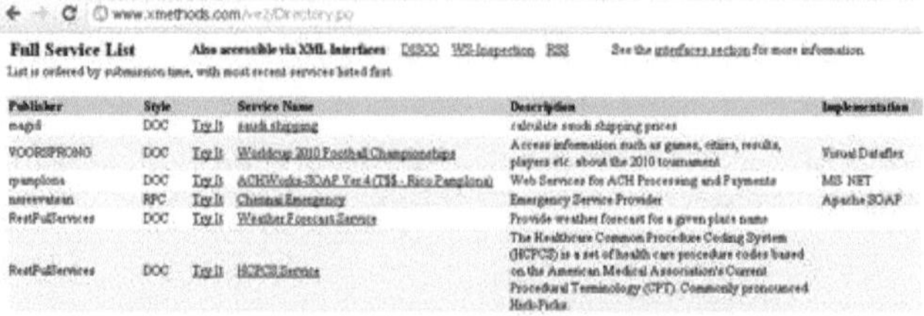

Figure 6. Some Web services published on Xmethods [4].

Although this directory is one of the first Web services publication registers, its main drawback is that it offers no automatic search mechanism for customers. They have to browse the list of Web services manually.

2.4.4.1.2 RemoteMethods

RemoteMethods[2] is a UDDI directory that enables Web services to be published, searched, discovered and classified, and includes around 380 Web services. According to [Legner 2007], RemoteMethods[2] was implemented in 1999 by *InfoGuinus inc.*
To publish a Web service on the site, the Web service provider must fill in an online form, which includes the name of the service, the name of the service provider, the name of the company that developed the service, the WSDL description and a text description. Adding other information such as the service price, the date of the last update and the duration of the devaluation period.
Once all the information on the form has been completed, it is submitted to the RemoteMethods[2] developers for approval and classification.
RemoteMethods[2] allows customers to recommend services. To recommend a web service, simply fill in an online form. The form includes the name of the recommended service, the service provider's website, the URL of the WSDL description and the e-mail address of the person recommending the service. Once the recommendation has been analysed by the RemoteMethods[2] developers, a decision will be taken to publish or reject the recommended Web service.
Web services on RemoteMethods[2] are classësed into eight catëgories, each catëgory is made up of preëëtablished sub-catëgories. Navigation between catëgories and sub-catëgories is via simple hyperlinks. Once the customer selects a catëgory, a list of services is displayed, containing the following information: service name, price, rating, date of last update. The customer can sort the list of services according to 1 of these attributes in an тащёге ascending or descending manner.

Figure 7. RemoteMethods web services access portal .[4]

Although RemoteMethods[2] allows customers to navigate between categories using simple hypertext links, it does not offer any means of searching for all the information characterising the services.

2.5 Quality of Service (*QoS*):

With the exponential increase in the use of Web services, the notion of quality of service has emerged in recent years and is becoming increasingly important for customers and service providers. Service selection has evolved rapidly, incorporating into the selection process not only functional information but also non-functional information (quality of service) such as performance, reliability, security, etc.

In this section, we discuss the concept of quality of service, its definition, its attributes and some service providers who integrate quality of service.

2.5.1 Definition

In the literature, there are several definitions of the concept of QoS. The ISO 9001:2000 standard defines quality as "*the totality of the characteristics of a product or service relating to its ability to satisfy implicit or explicit requirements*". This definition explains that good products or services are those that best satisfy these requirements.

[Vogel et al., 1995] defines quality of service as "*the set of quantitative and qualitative characteristics of a multimedia system, necessary to achieve the functionality required by the application*".

Another definition is given by [Robertson et al., 1999]: "*QoS are the properties that make the product more attractive, easier to use, faster or more reliable*". The authors specify that QoS properties are not mandatory, as they do not represent the main activity of the product, but they are recommended in order to describe the way in which its activities should be carried out.

[Ben Halima 2009] defines QoS as "*the attitude of a service to respond adequately to requirements, expressed or implicit, that aim to satisfy its users*". Several aspects can characterise these requirements, such as response time, capacity, availability, etc.

We can see that QoS is a set of non-functional requirements that aim to provide users with a means of finding the most relevant services among several other candidates that offer the same functionality.

2.5.2 Service quality models

In the literature, several models are proposedës to formalise the propertiesëtës of QoS, almost all of the proposed models are inspired by the first W3C model.

[4] http://www.remotemethods.com, latest access January 2017

2.5.2.1 Kangchan model

The World Wide Web Consostium (W3C) [**Kangchan et al., 2003**] has identified a set of properties for QoS: performance, reliability, scalability, capacity, robustness, exception handling, precision, integrity, accessibility, availability, interoperability, security and network QoS requirements.

S *Performance*: represents the speed with which a service request is completed. It is measured in terms of throughput, response time, latency, execution time, transaction time, etc.

S Reliability: represents the ability to perform its functions under specified conditions within a given timeframe, and is linked to the number of breakdowns per day, week or year.

s *Scalability*: represents the ability to increase the processing capacity of the service provider, and the ability to process more user requests in a given time. A scalable system must be able to ensure good performance as the number of requests to be processed increases.

s *Capacity*: this represents the number of requests that can be processed simultaneously.

s *Robustness*: represents the degree to which the service can function with the presence of invalid, incomplete or contradictory inputs.

s *Exception handling*: Web services must be provided with built-in exception handling functionality.

s *Accuracy*: defines the error rate produced by the service. The number of errors generated by the service must be minimised.

s *Integrity*: the integrity of the Web service must be provided in such a way that the system can prevent unauthorised access to the system's data or programmes.

s *Accessibility*: Web services must be provided with a high level of accessibility. It represents the service's ability to satisfy customer requests. Accessibility can be achieved through high scalability.

f *Availability*: the Web service must be ready for immediate use. It represents the probability that the system will be active. TTR (time-to-repair) indicates the time taken to repair a Web service, and is linked to availability.

f *Interoperability*: a Web service must be interoperable between the different development environments used to implement Web services.

f *Security*: the service provider must apply different approaches to provide services with a high level of security. Web services security means providing: authentication, authorisation, confidentiality, traceability, adaptability, encryption, etc.

2.5.2.2 Run model

Run [**Run 2003**] has organised QoS attributes into categories. Each category has a set of quantifiable and measurable parameters:

f Runtime-related QoS attributes: scalability, capacity, performance (response time, latency and throughput), reliability, availability, robustness, exception handling and accuracy.

f Attributes related to the transaction medium: transaction integrity.

f Configuration management price attributes: support standards, stability, price and completeness.

f Security attributes: authorisation, confidentiality, traceability, adaptability, encryption and non-repudiation.

2.5.2.3 Gwyduk model

The authors [**Gwyduk et al., 2006**] classify QoS into three categories: the system-level view, the service-level view and the business-level view.

f The system-level view: these are the qualities that have a relationship with Web services and platforms. The attributes of this level are :

o Interoperability: defines the level of interoperability of Web services. This attribute is described according to the following factors:

- Compliance: assesses the degree of compliance with standards.
- Interoperability: assesses whether the Web service is interoperable.

o Manageability: means the use of certain objects for quality management such as relationships between objects, identification, data status and structure, operations and ëvë Web services management events. This attribute is dëcribed according to the following factors:

- Introspection: provides information about Web service classes, resources and their states.
- Control: manages Web services and resources, including information obtained through introspection.
- Notification: notifies you of changes to the Web service or resource.
- Web service management: manages the web service itself.

o Business processing: business processing quality describes a set of indicators for optimising the business when business partners execute business processes using web services. To achieve high quality business processing, the following factors must be satisfied:

- Message reliability: represents the message delivery status.
- Collaboration: this factor refers to the state of business collaboration to combine, design and implement the business process.

o Security: represents the ability to ensure messages are not repudiated, authentication, confidentiality, etc.

S The service-level view: these are the qualities that can be seen by the user when using the service. The attributes of this level are: o Performance: represents the speed with which a service responds to a request. Performance is measured in terms of response time and maximum throughput.

- Response time: the amount of time between sending my request and receiving a response.
- Maximum throughput: the maximum number of services that can be processed by the service provider platform in a given period of time.

o Stability: represents the stability of the service in continuing to provide a service to customers. It is measured in terms of availability, accessibility and success.

- Availability: this is the ratio of the period of time during which the service exists and responds to customer requests.
- Accessibility: represents the degree to which a service is opëraйoпne1 to process messages without interruption.
- Successfulness: represents the degree to which customer request messages are successfully responded to without error.

S The business-level view: business-level attributes differentiate Web services according to business values. The attributes of this level are :

o Service charge: indicates the cost required to request the service.

o Degree of compensation: indicates the percentage of the exëcution price that will be reimbursed in the event that the service provider cannot honour its service commitment.

o Penalty rate: specifies the percentage of the performance price to be paid by the customer if the service order is cancelled.

o Reputation: measures confidence in the service, based on experience of different uses of the service.

2.5.3 QoS database: QWS Dataset

2.5.3.1 Presentation of QWS Dataset

The aim of this database [Al-Masri et al., 2007a] is to provide po881ЬIH1ё researchers in the field of Web services with a set of data for the expërimentation of their work. It is a database that provides a set of 365 real Web services that currently exist on the Web. A last update of this database includes a set of 2,507 Web services and their QWS metrics was performed in March 2008.

The Web services collected in QWS Dataset[5] are retrieved by a Web Service *Crawler* Engine (WSCE) [Al-Masri et al., 2007c], the majority of which are obtained from various sources such as UDDI registries, search engines and service portals. These services are then centralised in a single database called the QWS Dataset.

To search for a Web service within the QWS Dataset database, we need to base our search on service qualities. This will make it possible to find the most relevant Web services that best meet user prëfërences in terms of service quality. The service quality properties defined in this database are prësentëes in the following figure:

ID	Parameter Name	Description	Units
1	Response Time	Time taken to send a request and receive a response	ms
2	Availability	Number of successful invocations/total invocations	%
3	Throughput	Total Number of invocations for a given period of time	invokes/second
4	Successability	Number of response / number of request messages	%
5	Reliability	Ratio of the number of error messages to total messages	%
6	Compliance	The extent to which a WSDL document follows WSDL specification	%
7	Best Practices	The extent to which a Web service follows WS-I Basic Profile	%
8	Latency	Time taken for the server to process a given request	ms
9	Documentation	Measure of documentation (i.e. description tags) in WSDL	%
10	WsRF	Web Service Relevancy Function: a rank for Web Service Quality	%
11	Service Classification	Levels representing service offering qualities (1 through 4)	Classifier
12	Service Name	Name of the Web service	None
13	WSDL Address	Location of the Web Service Definition Language (WSDL) file on the Web	None

Figure 8. QWS Dataset quality of service properties .[6]

Response time: this is the time taken between the client sending the request and the Web service receiving the response. The unit of measurement is ms (milliseconds).

Availability: this is measured by the ratio between the number of successful invocations and the total number of invocations.

Throughput: this represents the number of invocations during a given period of time. The unit of measurement is (invocations/second).

Success: this is measured by the ratio between the number of responses and the number of requests.

Reliability: this is measured by the ratio between the number of error messages and the total number of messages.

Latency: this is the time taken by the server to process the message. The unit of measurement is ms (milliseconds).

2.5.3.2 Search function in QWS Dataset :

QWS Dataset offers a single keyword search method.

[5] http://www.uoguelph.ca/~qmahmoud/qws/index.html, last access September 2018.
[6] http://www.uoguelph.ca/~qmahmoud/qws/search. html last accessed September 2018.

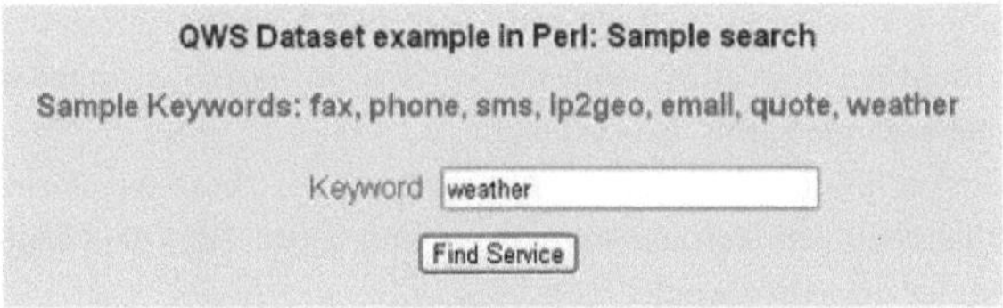

Figure 9. QWS Dataset search mask[7] .

The prěcědente search result returns all the Web services matching the query.

The QWS Dataset

Name	Response Time (ms)	Throughput (hits/sec)	Reliability (%)	Best Practices (%)	Documentation (%)	Class
FastWeather	125.44	13.5	96.4	90	91	★★★★
DOTSFastWeather	129.67	13.2	84.1	80	90	★★★★
WeatherForecast	261	1.8	58.1	80	94	★★★☆
WeatherFetcher	160	2.2	73.3	84	32	★★★☆
WeatherService	190.5	12.4	54	80	8	★★☆☆
GlobalWeather	1463.5	2.4	53.5	84	42	★★☆☆
ndfdXML	409.33	1.8	41.4	72	96	★☆☆☆

Figure 10. Search results from the previous example [6].

2.5.3.3 Classification of QWS Dataset services

The QWS Dataset service classification represents a set of service levels based on QoS. There are four classifications:

1. Platinum (High level)
2. Gold
3. Silver
4. Bronze (Low quality)

The classification is based on the quality offered by the service provided by WsRF. WsRF (Web service Relevancy Function) is a method developed by [Al-Masri et al., 2007b], which evaluates the quality of services from the lowest to the highest quality in the form of stars, from zero to four.

QWS Dataset offers services that are tested over three consecutive days, with test results obtained from two different networks. This database provides considerable support to researchers in the field of QoS. However, QWS Dataset is based on quality of service and neglects the functional part of services. Also, QWS Dataset does not offer rich search criteria, in fact the search is only done by keywords.

2.5.3.4 Disadvantages of QWS Dataset

According to [Kritikos et al., 2009], this database has a number of shortcomings, which are summarised below:

1- It provides the average value of each QoS attribute, not the minimum and maximum.

2- The number of QoS attributes (metrics) is fixed and small (execution time and throughput).

3- No means of accessing all the measurements taken for each service.

2.6 Conclusion

Web services are software entities that offer specific functions on the Web. The service description is used to give the customer all the information needed to use the service correctly. This information includes the service identifier, the inputs and outputs, the types of

[7] http://www.uoguelph.ca/~qmahmoud/qws/search. html last accessed September 2018.

data manipulated, the names of the operations and how to interact with each one. Communication between the client and the service is based on standards to simplify interoperability between platforms and systems.

Services are published in directories accessible on the Web. These directories enable service providers to publish their services and share them with users. They also enable customers to search for the web services they want.

The service description and publication standards that we have presented do not offer any information on service quality such as turnaround time, reliability, availability, etc. This information is very important for selecting the best services. This information is very important for selecting the best services.

In recent years, the Skyline operator has emerged as a new and popular paradigm for finding the most relevant Web services based on QoS data. In the next chapter, we present the Skyline method and its algorithms, as well as research work on Web service selection based on the Skyline method and its variants.

3 Selection of Skyline-based Web Services

In this chapter we introduce the concept of Skyline, then we present the basic algorithms of Skyline computation proposed in the literature, we will highlight the advantages and disadvantages of each algorithm, then, we present some variants of Skyline queries, we expose afterwards, the works that have adoptedës Skyline algorithms for the sëlection of Web services. At the end of this chapter, we will carry out a comparative ëtude between these works.

3.1 Introduction

The idëe of Skyline comes from early work on the contour probtome [McLainet al., 1974], the maximal vector [Kunget al., 1975] and the convex envelope [Preparata et al, 1985], it was first introduced in the domain of databases by [Borzsonyi et al., 2001]. Skyline is important for several applications that iK'cessitate multi-criteria decision making, such as databases and queries with user prëfërences [Benouaret et al., 2012b], ...etc. Taking a set of objects P1, P2, ...,Pn, the Skyline opërator returns all objects Pi, such that Pi is not dominated by any other object Pj. the Skyline relies on the Pareto dominance relation, dëfined as follows:

Taking Pi and Pj to be two points, Pi is said to dominate Pj, dënotë by Pi < Pj, if Pi is better than or ëequal to Pj on all attributes and better strictly on at least one attribute (we assume the best value is the smallest).

Vu E[1,m], Gu(Pi) < Gu(Pj) Л B v E[1,m], Gv(Pi) < Gv(Pj)

m: the number of criteria, Gu(Pi): the value of point Pi for criterion u.

An example of a query that demonstrates the relevance of the Skyline operator is that of finding the cheapest hotel closest to the beach in a database of donees.

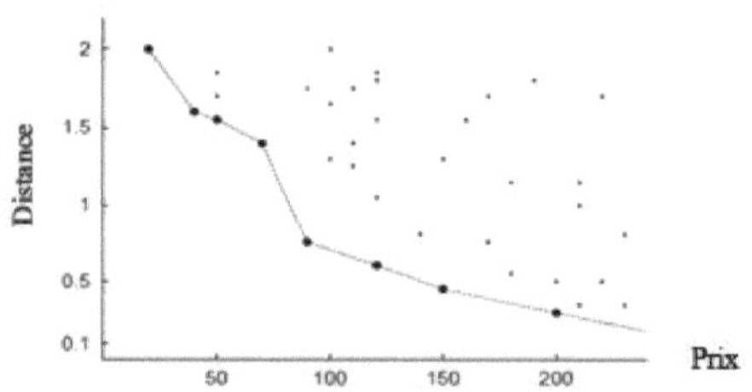

Prices

Figure 11. Skyline hotels [Borzsonyi et al., 2001].

Skyline computing has received considerable attention not only in database computing but also in other research areas such as service computing. The Skyline of a set of Web services contains those Web services that are not dominated by any other Web service on all QoS criteria. Several algorithms and Skyline variants have been proposed by OtO for the calculation of Skyline Web services.

3.2 Algorithms for calculating the Skyline

Skyline calculation algorithms available in the literature include: Block Nested Loop, Divide and Conquer, Bitmap, Index, Nearest Neighbor, Branch and Bound Skyline (BBS) and K-dominant-Skyline.

3.2.1 Block Nested Loop (BNL)

The Block Nested Loop (BNL) algorithm [Borzsonyi et al., 2001] is an itorative algorithm that scans the dataset over several iterations, in each iteration keeping a memory list of Skyline candidate points.

When a point is read, it is compared with the candidate points in memory. For each subsequent point, there are three possible cases:

1. If p is dominated by any point in the list, it is excluded from the Skyline result.
2. If p dominates any point in the list, it is inserted into the list, and all points in the list dominated by p are deleted.
3. If p is not dominated and does not dominate any list point, it is inserted into the list, and can be part of the Skyline list.

The list is auto-orgaпsëe, as each dominant point found6 is placë at the top of the list. This will reduce comparisons as each point that dominates several other points is pкcë first.

The proЬlëтe of 1 BNL algorithm is that the list can become larger than the mëmory [Papadias et al., 2003]. In this case, all the points ëcartës during the two ëtapes (1 and 2) will not increase the size of the list, but they will be placës in a temporary file. This requires several passes of BNL, in particular at the end of the scan of the data file, it is necessary to restart BNL using the point in the temporary file as inputs.

The advantage of the BNL lies in its wide use, since it can be used for all dimensions without indexing or ordering the data file. Its main drawbacks are that it relies on the central memory (a small memory requires several Orations), so it has to read all the data before returning the first Skyline results.

3.2.2 Divide and Conquer (D&C) :

The Divide and Conquer algorithm [Borzsonyi et al., 2001] goes through three ëtages to compute the Skyline result which are: divide, compute and merge.

1. Divide the set of points into m partitions $p_i, p_2, \ldots p_m$.
2. Calculate the Skyline s_i result for each p_i partition, using any Skyline calculation algorithm.
3. Merge the results of the m partitions to find the final result.

The D&C algorithm is effective for small databases, but for large databases partitioning requires reading and writing data at least once. Also, this algorithm cannot produce Skyline points progressively, as it cannot give any results until the end of the complete process.

3.2.3 Bitmap

The Bitmap algorithm [Tan et al., 2001], is proposed to ensure a progressive construction of Skyline results. The Bitmap sclwina asks the following question: "Is a point p dominated by another point?". If the answer is iregative, then that point p can be returned immediately. This algorithm can return Skyline points progressively, the response time is reduced compared to previous algorithms.

The Bitmap algorithm involves three tasks [Yu et al., 2010]: creating bit vectors, transforming bits into bit strings and calculating the Skyline result.

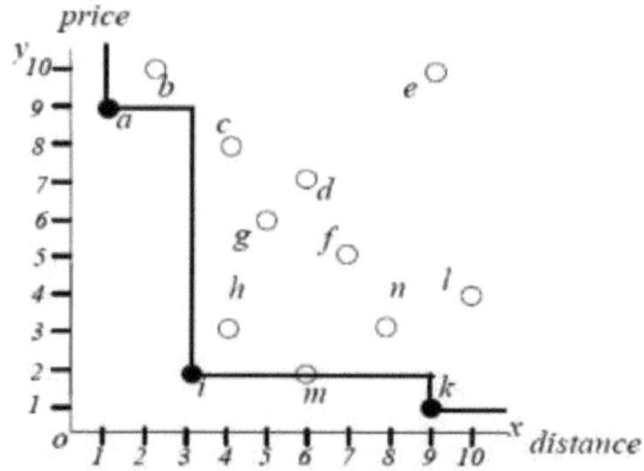

Figure 12. Example of a Skyline result [Papadias et al., 2003].

The Bitmap algorithm involves three tasks [Yu et al., 2010]: creating bit vectors, transforming bits into bit strings and calculating the Skyline result.

1. Creation of bit vectors: each data line x = (xi,x2,....,xd) of *d* dimensions is converted into a vector of m bits. m represents the number of different bits of all the dimensions. m = Ed=1 k_t , ki is the number of distinct values of the ith dimension. Done, x = (k1 bits, k2 bits, ..., kd bits).
2. Transformation of bit vectors into bit strings: instead of storing bit vectors individually, the Bitmap algorithm transposes bit vectors into an array of bit strings.
3. Skyline calculation: the algorithm uses the bit string array for the skyline calculation. Consider the data line *x = (Xi, X2,...., xd),* where xi is the jth distinct value in the ith dimension. The algorithm calculates C= *BSiji&...&BSdjd*, where & represents the logical operator "and". *BSj* represents the bit string for the ji®me distinct value of the i®me dimension. *BSj* contains n bits, where n is the total number of data records. After calculating C, the algorithm counts the number of "1's" in the bit string C. If C has two values equal to "1", then record x is not part of the Skyline result. The ime value equal to "1" in the C string corresponds to theme data record which dominates the x record.

id	coordinate	bitmap representation
a	(1,9)	(1111111111, 1100000000)
b	(2,10)	(1111111110, 1000000000)
c	(4,8)	(1111111000, 1110000000)
d	(6,7)	(1111100000, 1111000000)
e	(9,10)	(1100000000, 1000000000)
f	(7,5)	(1111000000, 1111110000)
g	(5,6)	(1111110000, 1111100000)
h	(4,3)	(1111111000, 1111111100)
i	(3,2)	(1111111100, 1111111110)
k	(9,1)	(1100000000, 1111111111)
l	(10,4)	(1000000000, 1111111000)
m	(6,2)	(1111100000, 1111111110)
n	(8,3)	(1110000000, 1111111100)

Figure 13. Example of the Bitmap representation [Papadias et al., 2003].

In the example in figure 12, to find out whether point C (1111111000, 1110000000) belongs to the Skyline result, the algorithm creates the bit string Cx= 1110000110000 and Cy= 0011011111111, by juxtaposing the 4eme and 8eme corresponding bits (see figure 13). Calculating Cx&Cy = 0010000110000, this result indicates that point c is dominated by points 8 and 9 (*h* and *i*).

The effectiveness of the Bitmap algorithm lies in binary operations. This algorithm can quickly return the first Skyline points, taking into account their insertion orders. The disadvantage of this algorithm is that it cannot adapt to user preferences, which is an important criterion for a good Skyline algorithm. Also, the complete calculation of the Skyline is very expensive, because, for each point tested, it has to use the bitmaps of all the other points to get the juxtaposition. It is also not suitable for dynamic data sets, as insertion can change the order of attribute values.

3.2.4 Index

The algorithm proposed by [Tan et al., 2001] is based on the B-tree. It proposes a transformation mechanism that converts points with several dimensions into a single value, this transformation organises the data space into different partitions based on the dimensions with the largest values and orders each partition. After this transformation, each dimension can be indexed using the value from the transformation. The rest of the calculation is done as follows:

1. Find the first Skyline point: the algorithm scans the indexes in parallel to find the first Skyline point on all dimensions. This first point is definitive and can be returned to the client.
2. Remove non-Skyline points: take the index of the first dimension and scan the rest of the index entries after the returned Skyline point. If the entries after this Skyline point are dominated on all dimensions, then these points will not form part of the Skyline result and must be deleted.
3. Calculate the Skyline result for the rest of the points: for the other points which have lower or higher index entries than the returned points. Skyline algorithms are applied to produce other Skyline results.

An improved version of this algorithm is proposed by [Papadias et al., 2003], in which points in *d* dimensions are organised into *d* lists, with the point p =(p_1, p_2, ..., p_d) being assigned to list number *i* (1 < i < d), if and only if its p_i strings in axis number *i* are the minimum on all dimensions. The points in each list are sorted in ascending order, according to their minimum strings, and indexed using a B-tree. This operation allows the first Skyline points to be returned quickly and facilitates the elimination of non-Skyline points.

list 1		list 2	
a (1, 9)	*minC*=1	*k* (9, 1)	*minC*=1
b (2, 10)	*minC*=2	*i* (3, 2), *m* (6, 2)	*minC*=2
c (4, 8)	*minC*=4	*h* (4, 3), *n* (8, 3)	*minC*=3
g (5, 6)	*minC*=5	*l* (10, 4)	*minC*=4
d (6, 7)	*minC*=6	*f* (7, 5)	*minC*=5
e (9, 10)	*minC*=9		

Figure 14. Example of representation in Index [Papadias et al., 2003].

The main advantage of the Index algorithm lies in its ability to quickly return the first Skyline points to the head of the lists, but it has the same disadvantage as the Bitmap: the order of the Skyline points is fixed and it does not support user preferences.

3.2.5 Nearest Neighbor (NN)

The Skyline Nearest Neighbor (NN) algorithm [Kossmannet al., 2002] [Papadias et al., 2003], uses the result of the Nearest Neighbor algorithm to recursively partition the data. NN performs the query using an R-tree to find the points that have minimal distances (mindist) from the starting point of the axes (point 0). The mindist of a point p ёдаle has the sum of the strings of p. It can be shown that the first Nearest Neighbor point is part of the Skyline result.

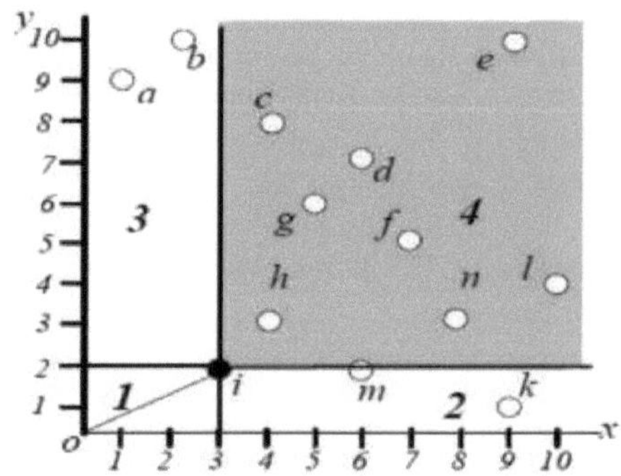

Figure 15. First Skyline point with NN [Papadias et al., 2003].

The Skyline result is calculated as follows:

1. Calculate the nearest neighbour at the starting point of the (0,0) axes. The point returned in the previous example $p1 = \{i\}$ is a point which is part of the Skyline result, and can be returned immediately to the client.
2. Divide the space into different partitions. The partition between point 0 and the first Skyline point *p1* must be empty (Partition 1 in Figure 11). The points in partition 4 are all dominated by p1, so they are removed from the calculation process. Partitions 2 and 3 will be treated as new partitions. They are inserted into the TO-DO list.
3. For each partition in the TO-DO list, apply steps 1 and 2 until the TO-DO list is empty.

According to [Papadias et al., 2003] NN is faster up to 4 dimensions compared to the previous algorithms, in particular NN returns the whole Skyline result faster than the Index and this difference increases with the size of the Skyline. On the other hand, the Index performs better for the progressive return of Skyline results. For more than 03 dimensions, the cost of NN increases due to the increase in the overlap space between partitions. In this case, index is not applicable due to the large space requirement. D&C and Bitmap are not favoured, as the costs of merging and loading the bitmap are not advantageous. BNL can produce small skylines, but the cost increases as the size of the skyline result increases due to the high number of iterations required.

3.2.6 Branch and Bound Skyline (BBS)

The BBS algorithm [Papadias et al., 2003], [Papadias et al., 2005] is based on the same principle as NN, it uses a stack to determine the order of data retrieval and the R-tree index:

1- BBS traverses the entries of the R-tree (leaves and intermediaries) in ascending order of their distances from the 0 axis.

2- Each point added to the Skyline list during the execution of the algorithm is guaranteed to remain in the final list of Skyline points.

3- For each point examined, at least one of its ancestor nodes is removed from the stack.

Let's take the example of the Error! Source of the reference not found., BBS starts from the root node of the R-tree, it inserts the entry e7 which is the minimum in mindist, then it inserts the entry e6. The minimum mindist entry (e7) is expanded, deleting entry e7 and inserting its children (e3, e4, e5) into the stack, the nearest neighbour in the stack is e3 which contains the mindist (i = 5), e3 is removed from the stack and replaced by the leaves, (g,11), (h,7),(i,5), and as i dominates h and g, it is the first Skyline point, so it is inserted into the list of Skyline points.

The stack contains the elements (e6, e4, e5), the mindist of e6 is the minimum, so e6 is replaced in the stack by its children e1 and e2. The stack thus contains (e1, e2, e4, e5), e2 and e5 are dominated by i they are discarded. The mindist is e1 (mindist =8), p1 is replaced by its leaves, so the stack will contain (a, b, e4), a dominates b, so b is removed from the stack, a is not dominated by i, so a is added to the Skyline list. The remaining element e4 is extended, (k, l), point k dominates point l, so delete l. point k is not dominated by the Skyline points (i and a) so add point k to the Skyline list.

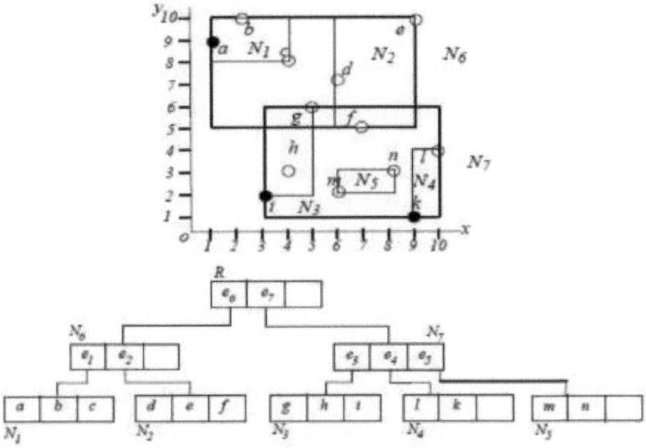

Figure 16. Example of an R-tree.

3.3 Skyline variants

One of the major drawbacks of Skyline is that when the number of dimensions is very large, the size of the Skyline result becomes larger and no longer offers interesting perspectives [Chan et al., 2006]. To overcome this inconvënient, several dërivëes variants of the Skyline have ële proposëes including: k-dominant Skyline, K-repr'sentative Skyline, Frequence

Skyline and Top-k dominating Skyline.

3.3.1 K-dominant Skyline

The k-dominant Skyline variant has ëlë proposëe by [Chan et al. 2006]. Given a data set of *d* dimensions. A point *p* k-dominates another point *q*, if there exist *k* (*k*<*d*) dimensions in which p is better or 'gal a *q* and better in at least one of the *d* dimensions. A point which is not k-dominated by any of the other points is returned in the K-dominant Skyline result.

The other Skyline calculation algorithms presented earlier are not easily adaptable to find K-dominant Skylines. This is due to the transitive property of the dominance relation of the original Skyline, which is no longer considered k-dominant.

For any *k*<*d*, it is possible to have three points *p, q, r* such that *p* k-dominates *q*, *q* k-dominates *r* and *r* k-dominates *p*, forming a cyclic dominance relationship. Therefore, one point cannot be 'carved out' during processing, even if that point is k-dominant, because that particular point can be used to exclude another point through a k-dominant relationship. Existing Skyline calculation algorithms do not satisfy this requirement.

3.3.2 K-representative Skyline

Given that the size of the Skyline result cannot be controlled, the K-representative Skyline concept has been proposed to reduce this result, by returning only the most relevant points. It consists of segmenting the Skyline result into a set of clusters and returning a single point from each cluster that best represents it. [Lin et al., 2007] proposes an approach for calculating the k-representative Skyline return where each cluster is represented by a single point, so that the number of points dominated is maximised. For the calculation of top-k representative Skyline queries, the authors propose an algorithm using the FM (Flajolet and Martin probabilistic counting technique) proposed by [Flajolet et al., 1985]. On the other hand, [Tao et al., 2009] proposed a distance-based approach to compute the representative Skyline Top-k and to choose from each cluster the Skyline point that has the best compromise between the criteria; the authors proposedë a computational algorithm that computes the representative Skyline points directly without going through the computation of the total Skyline result; according to the authors, a better approach is to return a few Skyline points quickly representing the contour of the global Skyline result. Three algorithms have ële adoptedës for computing Skyline representative top-k: the Naive- greedy algorithm [Feder et al., 1988] first computes the Skyline result before computing the Skyline K-representative by computing the distance between Skyline points; the I-greedy algorithm [Beckmann et al., 1990] is an efficient implementation of Naive-greedy, based on an R-tree; the Best-first algorithm [Hjaltason et al., 1999] returns representative Skylines without calculating the full Skyline result.

3.3.3 Frequence Skyline

The concept of Skyline frequency was proposed by [Chan et al., 2006b], it measures the number of subspaces where a point p is a Skyline point, then the number of subspaces where p is a Skyline point are added together to calculate the Skyline frequency. It takes a very long time to calculate the Skyline result for each subspace.

According to [Vlachou et al., 2010], the disadvantage of this variant is that all Skyline points that appear in the same subspace have the same Skyline frequency. In addition, it favours extreme Skyline points that are better on only one dimension, whereas the objective of Skyline is to return points that have a good compromise between all dimensions.

3.3.4 Top-k dominating Skyline

Queries with prëfërences have attracted attention in the database field, in particular, two types

of queries that have gained more importance and have been studied in depth: top-k and Skyline queries. With Top-k queries, the user provides a ranking function to order objects according to their scores and return to the user the best top-k objects, however, Skyline returns the set of objects that are not domiiK's. The most important advantage of a top-k query is that the number of results is limited, which is not true for Skyline queries [Tiakas et al., 2007]. Top-k dominating Skyline combines the advantages of Top-k and Skyline queries with ëHш^я!: their disadvantages by assigning each object a low intuitive scoreë on dominance.
Some algorithms have been proposed to compute Top-k dominating queries, [Papadias et al., 2005] proposed a Skyline-Based Top-k Dominating Algorithm (STD) inspired by the Branch-and-Bound Skyline (BBS) algorithm. [Yiu et al., 2007] proposed the Iterative Top-k Dominating Algorithm (ITD), an optimised version of STD, which reduces the computation time and is based on an R-tree structure.

3.3.5 Skyrank

According to [Vlachou et al., 2010], Skyline aims to help users make intelligent dëcisions on complex data by dëcovering the most intëressful set of points, in particular, when there are many criteria and conflicting Skyline points. However, as the dimensionality of the data set increases, the Skyline operator loses its efficiency by returning a large proportion of the data, which makes it very difficult for users to make decisions. Users need a tidy list of the most relevant Skyline points. The authors have proposed a framework called SKYRANK for arranging Skyline points, with or without a function that defines the user's prëfërences. SKYRANK is based on the 'Skyline graph', which defines the dominance relationships between Skyline points for subsets of dimensions. To demonstrate the effectiveness of this approach, an experimental study was carried out on real data (NBA and DBLP) and on synthetic data. The results were compared with the approaches [Chan et al., 2006b] and [Tao et al., 2009].

3.4 Selection of Web Services Bases on the Skyline

Several works have been proposed in the literature that use a variety of Skyline algorithms for Web service selection and composition.
In the thesis of [Benouaret 2012], the author addresses several issues related to the selection of Skyline Web services, namely, the selection of majority Skyline Web services, the consideration of user preferences for the optimization and composition of Web services, the optimization of Web service selection for multiple users with conflicting preferences, the selection of services with a good compromise between QoS attributes and the consideration of the uncertainty aspect of QoS data, during the Skyline service selection process. [Benouaret et al., 2012a] proposed a Framework called WS-Sky for QoS-based Web services selection, a Skyline variant was presented called o- dominant Skyline for the ordering of Skyline Web services considered incomparable, also, this variant allows to reduce the size of the Skyline result when needed. In the work of [Benouaret et al., 2012b], the Skyline collective concept was proposed to address the problem of multiple user preferences; to determine the relevance of each Web service, a degree' of matching a ëlë calcиlë between user prëfërences and service constraints.
For the sëlection of Web services with multiple prëfërences, [Benouaret et al., 2012c] introduced the *Majority Skyline* concept, this concept is dëfined as follows: Let Ube *a* set of users, s_i and s_j be two Web services. We say that s_i dominates majority s_j if only if there exists a subset *U'* belongs to *U,* such that *U'* contains more than the пюШё of users, knowing that s_i

dominates s_j (s_i has a better binding degree than s_j for l'user u_i on all prëfërences spëcifiëes) for all users of subset *U'*. A spëcific characteristic *of Skyline majority* is that a majority dominated service will not be ëcartedë as it can be иШ18ё for ёcaJleг other services. For efficient computation of the majority Skyline services, the author adapts the two algorithms OSA (One Scan Algorithm) and TSA (Two Scan Algorithm) [Chan et al. 2006].

In another work in [Benouaret et al., 2011], 1 author explains that the service Skyline computation privileges services with a poor trade-off between QoS criteria, and the size of the Skyline result can be very large, requiring a lot of effort from users. To remëdier these inconvënients, the author adopts the fuzzy dominance opërator for Skyline Web service computation:

Given s_i, s_j two Web services, the fuzzy dominance relation is usedëe to express the degree to which s_i dominates s_j.

An algorithm (a-DSSA: Dominance Service Skyline Algorithm) has 't' propos' for calculating fuzzy, low-level service skylines on an index structure and an R-tree.

Motivated by this work, [Halfaoui et al., 2015] proposed an approach based on the notion of 'Fuzzy dominated Score', which allows Skyline Web services considered as incomparable in the Skyline sense (Pareto dominance) to be ranked. The authors propose to rank incomparable Skyline Web services using a relationship called '*is dominated by*', which is the inverse of the Pareto '*is dominant*' relationship [Halfaoui 2017]. It associates each web service with the number of services that dominate it. To evaluate the performance of this approach, a comparative study with the approach of [Benouaret et al., 2011] was carried out, using the database [Al-masri et al., 2007].

In another work by [Benouaret et al., 2012c], the problem of calculating Skyline services from uncertain QoS data was addressed, according to the authors, QoS values can change over time which does not reflect the actual performance of Web services. For example, response time and data rate can vary depending on the quality of the network between the client and the service provider. Skyline computation of uncertain QoS data therefore becomes a very important task. The authors have introduced two new concepts: *pos-dominant* Skyline service for calculating the possibility of one service dominating another, and *nec-dominant* Skyline service for calculating the likelihood of one service dominating another, in order to make it easier for the user to select the desired Web services taking into account the presence of uncertain QoS data. The two new concepts are based on possibility theory to extend the dominance relation in the case of uncertain QoS. The Two Scan Algorithm (TSA) [Chan et al. 2006] is adapted to implement the two concepts of *post-dominant* Skyline service and *nec-dominant* Skyline service.

[Yu et al., 2009] The authors adapt existing Skyline algorithms to calculate the best SEP (Service Execution Plan). The Skyline result of the SEPs, represents the set of SEPs that are not dominated by other SEPs. In this contribution, two algorithms are proposed (BBS4SEP and OGI) to compute the Skyline service.

- BBS4SEP algorithm: this is an extension to the BBS (Branch and Bound Skyline) algorithm by implementing a few changes to BBS. The BBS4SEP algorithm is capable of efficiently calculating Skyline SEPs.
- OGI algorithm (Operation Graph based Indexing): this is an improvement on the BBS4ESP algorithm, and consists of running it on an indexed R-tree built on the basis of ESP spaces. OGI offers the following advantages:

1. Automatic generation of the SEP space for each service request ;

2. The R-tree index on the SEP space has a low dimension compared to the R-tree of the original space.

In the paper proposed by [Yu et al., 2010a], the authors propose two algorithms, OPA and DPA, in addition to a BUA heuristic approach, to select the best composite services.

1. OPA (One Pass Algorithm): During a single iteration in the SEP space, it lists SEP candidates one by one, and records only potential SEPs. The Skyline result is returned after all candidate SEPs have been examined.

2. DPA (Dual Progressive Algorithm): ADP progressively lists the MEPs (Multiple services Execution Plans), in ascending order of their scores. This enables the Skyline result to be returned progressively. This is because each MEP discovered last cannot have a lower score than the MIP previously discovered.

3. BUA (Bottom-Up Approach): this is a heuristic approach proposed to optimise the performance of the DPA algorithm. The performance of DPA is related to the size of the MEP space and the size of the stack. As the number of services increases, the space required will be equally important for both.

In another work by the same authors [Yu et al, 2010b], two limitations have ël.ë raisedë on current optimization approaches, the first limitation is that most existing approaches are consideredërëes as black boxes, where the user has to send his weights of QoS parameters to the server, which makes the sëlection and sends the result back to the user without any flexibility to choose the services dësirësed by the user himself. The second limitation is that current approaches assume that the quality of service delivered does not change over time. However, QoS values do not accurately reflect actual service performance. This is because performance can change due to the dynamic environment of services e.g. response time and data rate can vary due to the quality of the computer network or the internet network. Therefore, the quality of service provided by service providers is uncertain.

To overcome these limitations, a new concept called *p-dominant Skyline service* has ëlë introduced.

p-dominant Skyline: incorporating QoS uncertainty into Skyline service analysis gives users an in-depth understanding of service provider behaviour in a dynamic environment.

A supplier S belongs to the p-dominant Skyline if the probability of S being dominated by another supplier is less than p, pe [0,1].

For the calculation of p-dominant-Skyline, the proposed algorithm is based on a new indexing structure, called *p-R-tree*. P-R-tree makes it possible to efficiently discard uncertain objects that are p-dominated by other objects.

According to [Dai et al., 2013], Skyline can help determine the optimal allocation of weights to different mëtrics. Based on the Skyline dominance relation, the number of candidate services can be reduced and the selection process can be simplified. A new concept is introduced called dominance degree, which can capture the dominance scale of Skyline Web services and orders Skyline results by dominance degree.

In the work of [Alrifai et al., 2010], the authors propose an approach for the sëlection of Skyline Web services in order to prepare them for a composition phase. The objective is to reduce 1 search space by focusing only on Web services that are not dominos. To aтëHorer the performance of this approach, it has ël.ë proposë to perform the Skyline computation step in Offline, in case of addition or deletion of a Web service, the Skyline result is recalculo automatically. To overcome the problem of the large size of the Skyline result, the authors propose segmenting it into a set of clusters and selecting a single representative service from each cluster. Five methods were used to select Skyline Web services with a view to composing them:

- Exact: uses the MIP (Mixer Integer proramming) optimisation technique to select Web services without using Skyline ;
- ExactSkyline: similar to the Exact method, except that it only takes Skyline web services into account;
- SkylineRep: this method starts by performing a hiorarchical clustering on the Skyline rosultat and taking a single Skyline service from each cluster as omitting a reprosentative service.
- Hybrid: uses the MIP method for global optimization of Web services [Alrifai et al., 2009] .
- HybridSkyline: similar to the hybrid method, except that it is applied to reprosentative Skyline web services.

To demonstrate the efficiency of these methods, the authors used the real database proposed by [El-masri et al., 2007] and three synthetic databases: correlated, anti-correlated and independent. When comparing the Exact and ExactSkyline methods, a significant improvement in performance was observed when the search space was restricted to Skyline web services. This improvement also depended on the type of database used. In other words, the authors found that the HybridSkyline method performed better than the other methods.

[Skoutas et al., 2010] propose two approaches for the discovery and selection of Web services. The first approach is a ranking methodology for Web services relevant to a given query, introducing objective measures based on defined dominance relationships between Web services; three ranking algorithms have been used:

- Dominated score: The aim is to quickly find the set of objects that dominate each object.
- Dominating score: this captures the objects that dominate the greatest number of other objects.
- Dominance score: a ranking score which calculates a compromise between the dominance score and the dominant score.

The second approach exploits methods for segmenting relevant services in a way that reflects the different trade-offs between parameters. Two clustering algorithms have been proposed: the first called ASC (Approximate Skyline Clustering) is an improved version of greedy [Tao et al., 2009], and the second called HSC (Heuristic Skyline Clustering) which starts with the basic idea of avoiding the most expensive searches.

[Chen et al., 2010] proposed an approach for the selection of representative Skyline Web services, they propose a method based on a similarity measure to compute representative Skyline Web services. Assuming that a point p is a Skyline point, if the distance between point p and point q is no longer than 1, we call the two points p and q 1-similar points. In this way, Skyline Web Services are segmented into a set of 1-similar clusters. The final step is to use the covering circle method to select the most representative point from each 1-similar cluster. To demonstrate the effectiveness of this approach, the authors compared the results with those of the two approaches proposed by [Lin et al., 2007] and [Tao et al., 2009].

[Bouanaka et al., 2013] have proposed an approach consisting of three steps: (i) Web services are classified according to their functionalities, (ii) the Skyline function is applied to each class to select only the most relevant Web services for the next step, (iii) a utility function is used to evaluate the overall multidimensional qualities of a given service, by aggregating the QoS vector into a single value.

The authors in [Kumar et al., 2016] started by grouping web services that have similar QoS into a set of clusters, then Skyline is applied on each cluster to eliminate the dominant web services and return only the relevant web services.

3.5 Summary of Skyline-based Web Services Selection Work In the table below, we have carried out a comparative study of the different approaches to Skyline Web services selection. We have considered the following criteria:

- The name of the Skyline variant
- The basic ий^ë algorithm for the Skyline calculation.
- The dominance relationship used (strict, fuzzy or probabilistic)
- Support for the importance of sëlection criteria
- Taking account of user preferences
- Handling uncertainty in QoS data

From the comparative table below (Table 1), we can see that the Skyline operator has attracted a lot of attention in the Service Computing community, where several approaches based on the Skyline and its variants have been proposed, in particular for optimising the selection of Web services.

We have noticed that some works have proposed new Skyline variants to address specific needs such as: o-dominant [Benouaret et al., 2011] and p- dominant [Yu et al, 2010b] for computing Skyline Web services on uncertain QoS data; Collective Skyline [Benouaret et al., 201b] and Majority Skyline [Benouaret et al., 2012c] for handling conflicting prëfërences of multiple users. Other work has focused on the progressive return of Skyline results [Yu et al., 2010a] proposing specific Skyline algorithms.

Other studies have proposed replacing the strict Skyline dominance relation by other dominance relations such as fuzzy dominance [Benouaret et al., 2012d] [Halfaoui et al., 2015], dominance probability [Yu et al., 2010b], or dominance degree [Dai et al., 2013]. This is to satisfy certain objectives such as: dealing with uncertainty in QoS data or taking user preferences into account.

We have noticed that there is little research based on Skyline that takes into account the importance of QoS criteria, given that Skyline gives the same level of importance to all QoS criteria. However, this differs from one domain to another, for example in the electronic payment domain, the security criterion is more important than the other QoS criteria.

Furthermore, we have found that Skyline is used in some studies to reduce the search space in order to focus on Web services that are not dominated by any other Web service [Elrifai et al., 2010], [Dai et al., 2013] [Kumar et al., 2016].

Table 1. Comparison of service selection approaches based on Skyline.

Approach	Skyline variant	Algorithm	Dominance relationship	Importance of the criteria	User preferences	l'uncertainty QoS data
[Benouaret et al., 2012a]	G-dominant Skyline	Base on BBS	Blur	No	No	Yes
[Benouaret et al., 201b]	Collective Skyline	-	Strict	No	Yes	No
[Benouaret et al., 2012c]	Majority Skyline	-	Strict	No	Yes	No
[Benouaret et al., 2012d]	Pos-dominant Nec-dominant	TSA (two Scan Algorithm)	Blur	No	No	Yes
[Benouaret et al., 2011]	a-dominant Skyline	Base on BBS	Blur	No	No	Yes
[Halfaoui et al., 2015]	AFDetS	Base on SFS	Blur	No	No	Yes

[Yu et al., 2009]	SEP Skyline	BBS OGI	Strict	No	No	No
[Yu et al., 2010a],	Skylines multiservice	TAKEOVER BID DPA	Strict	No	No	No
[Yu et al., 2010b]	p-dominant Skyline	TPA	Probability of dominance	No	No	Yes
[Dai et al., 2013]	Degree of dominance	Skyline	Degree of dominance	No	Yes	Yes
[Alrifai et al., 2010],	Representative Skyline	Skyline + Clustering	Strict	Yes	No	No
[Skoutas et al., 2010]	Top-k domianting	Clustering + Top-k domianting	Strict	No	No	No
[Chen et al., 2010]	Similarity based Representative Skyline	SBRSA	Strict	No	No	No
[Bouanaka et al., 2013]	Skyline	BBS and BNL	Strict	No	No	No
[Kumar et al., 2016]	Skyline	Clustering + BNL	Strict	No	No	No

3.6 Conclusion

In this chapter we have presented the Skyline operator and its various variants and calculation algorithms, as well as the research work on Skyline-based selection of Web services.

The Skyline operator is very important for several domains that require multi-objective decision making. A point p is considered to be a Skyline point if p is better than or equal to all other points on all dimensions and p is better strictly than all other points on at least one dimension. There are many algorithms for calculating Skyline queries, and we have presented those that represent the basic algorithms, namely: BNL, D&C, index, Bitmap, NN, BBS; for each algorithm, we have presented its strengths and weaknesses.

Recently, Skyline has gained a lot of attention in the Services Oriented Computing (SOC) community, several works have been proposed for the optimisation of selection and web services based on Skyline algorithms and variants. We have noted that some work has proposed new Skyline variants to meet specific needs such as: computing Skyline web services on uncertain QoS data; handling conflicting preferences of multiple users; and progressively returning Skyline results. However, there is little research based on Skyline that takes into account the importance of QoS criteria, given that Skyline gives the same level of importance to all QoS criteria.

In the next chapter, we will focus on research into the contribution of multi-criteria decision support methods (MCDMs) to the selection of Web services.

4 Web Services Selection Based on MCDM Methods

The sëlection of Web services, which have similar functionalities with different service qualities is dëfmie as ëtant a proЬlëre of multicriteria decision support [Elrifai et al., 2010]. Several MCDM methods have been proposed in the literature in order to offer the user a set of tools to choose an alternative among several possible candidates.

In this chapter, we present the most widely used multicriteria decision support methods for weighting QoS criteria and selecting Web services, in particular AHP, fuzzy AHP and Prometheus. Next, we cite research works that use or adopt multicriteria decision support methods (MCDMs) for the weighting of QoS criteria and the selection of Web services. We conclude with a comparative study between these different approaches based on certain criteria.

4.1 Multi-criteria Decision Support Methods (MCDM)

Multicriteria decision making is one of the most important branches of operations research whose goal is to design mathematical and computational tools to select the best alternative among several criteria by a single decision maker or by a group of decision makers [Mohammadshahi et al., 2013]. Multi-criteria decision support methods (MCDM) is a collection of methodologies for comparing, ranking and selecting alternatives, each with several attributes. This depends on a matrix called the evaluation matrix or the decision matrix [Whaiduzzaman et al., 2014]. MCDM methods can be used to:

- Weighting of criteria: weighting methods allow users to express their preferences in relation to the criteria in order to quantify the importance of the weight of each criterion.
- Ranking alternatives: the principle behind these methods is to rank or classify alternatives according to their performance.

Note that certain weighting methods can be used to rank alternatives such as AHP and its variants.

4.2 Weighting methods

Criterion weighting is a very important step in the decision making process, it quantifies 1 importance of crores by exploiting 1 user preferences or 1 history data. In the literature there are several criterion weighting mëthods [Almulla et al., 2015] [Lahby 2013], they are classified into two categories; the first category represent subjective weighting methods; they consist in making preferences explicit to calculate criterion weights. These methods include: AHP [Saaty 1987], ANP [Saaty 1996] and AHP Floue [Laarhoven 1983] [Buckley 1985][Chang 1996].

The second category represents objective weighting methods, which use data to assign weights to criteria. Objective weighting methods include entropy [Shannon 1948], FDCW (Fuzzy Distance Correlation Weighting) [Almulla 2011] and genetic algorithms [Goldberg 1988].

In this section we present AHP and Fuzzy AHP as subjective weighting methods and entropy as an objective weighting method.

4.2.1 AHP (Analytic Hierarchy Process)

AHP is a multi-criteria decision support method developed by [Saaty 1987], it is frequently used by decision-makers in the comparison between objectives or alternatives, it allows the subjectivity of the decision-maker to be integrated in the form of weights. The AHP method decomposes the multi-criteria decision-making problem in the form of a hierarchical structure, this hierarchical structure reflecting the natural tendency and mindset of human beings. AHP starts with binary comparison matrices and, after a series of computational operations, arrives at a weight vector.

4.2.1.1 Steps in the AHP Method

The steps of the AHP method are [Lahby 2013]:

1- Step 1: Break down the problem into a hierarchical structure, with the objective at the top of the hierarchy, the criteria and sub-criteria that contribute to achieving the objective at the middle level, and the alternatives at the last level.

2- Step 2: Compare the elements of each hierarchical level in pairs and construct the comparison matrices.

The overall form of a comparison matrix is :

$$X = \begin{pmatrix} x_{11} & x12 & \dots & x_{1n} \\ x_{21} & x_{22} & \dots & x_{2n} \\ \dots & \dots & \dots & \dots \\ x_{n1} & x_{n2} & \dots & x_{nn} \end{pmatrix} \quad avec\ x_{ij} = \begin{cases} 1 & si\ i = j \\ \frac{1}{x_{ij}} & si\ i \neq j \end{cases} \qquad (4.1)$$

The values of these matrices are obtained by transforming the subjectivity of the decision-maker into numerical values using Saaty's scale:

Table 2. Saaty scale of the AHP method [Saaty 1987].

Degree of importance	**Definition**
1	Equal importance of the two elements
3	Low importance of one element in relation to another.
5	Strong or determining importance of one element in relation to another.
7	Proven importance of one element in relation to another.
9	Absolute importance of one element in relation to another.
2,4,6,8	Intermediate values between two similar assessments

3- Step 3: Normalise the comparison matrix using the following formulae

$$a_{ij} = \frac{x_{ij}}{\sum_{1}^{n} x_{ij}} \qquad (4.2)$$

$$A = \begin{pmatrix} a_{11} & a12 & \dots & a_{1n} \\ a_{21} & a_{22} & \dots & a_{2n} \\ \dots & \dots & \dots & \dots \\ a_{n1} & a_{n2} & \dots & a_{nn} \end{pmatrix} \qquad (4.3)$$

4- Step 4: Determine the relative importance of each element

$$W_i = \frac{\sum_{j-1}^{n} a_{ij}}{n} \quad et \sum_{i-1}^{n} W_i = 1 \qquad (4.4)$$

Or: n represents the number of dldments to compare.

5- Step 5: To check the coherence of the user's judgements, two indices were introduced by Saaty [Saaty 1987]: coherence index (CI) and coherence ratio (CR).

- Calculating the cohesion index

$$CI = \frac{\lambda_{max} - n}{n-1} \qquad (4.5)$$

- Calculation of λ_{max}

$$\lambda_{max} = \frac{\sum_{i-1}^{n} b_i}{n-1} \; sachant\, que\, b_i = \frac{\sum_{j-1}^{n} W_i * a_{ij}}{W_i} \qquad (4.6)$$

knowing thatb

- Calculating the coherence ratio

$$RC = \frac{IC}{ACI} \qquad (4.7)$$

Or: ACI (Average Coherence Indication) represents the average cohërence index obtained from the following table:

Table 3. Average coherence index.

Dimension of the matrix	1	2	3	4	5	6	7	8	9	10
ACI	0.00	0.00	0.58	0.90	1.12	1.24	1.32	1.41	1.45	1.49

According to Saaty, a CR value of less than 10% means that the user's judgements are accepted. If this value exceeds 10%, the user must revise his judgements.

6- Step 6: Calculation of the eigenvectors and priorities of the alternatives

The last step consists in calculating the global priorities of the alternatives in order to obtain a total ranking of the alternatives, according to the following formula [Ennaceur 2015] :

$$A_i = \sum_{j-1}^{n} V_{ij} * W_j \qquad (4.8)$$

Where: v_{ij} describes the performance of alternative Ai according to criterion j, and w_j describes the weight of criterion j.

4.2.1.2 Advantages and disadvantages of the AHP method

[Ennaceur 2015] summarized the following benefits for AHP:

- This is the only method known to MCDM that can measure the consistency of user judgements;
- It can also help users to organise the critical aspects of a problem into a hierarchical structure, making the decision-making process easy to manage;
- Pairwise comparisons in AHP are often preferred by decision-makers, allowing them to calculate criterion weights and tens of alternatives from the comparison matrices rather than quantifying the weights/scores directly.
- The AHP method can be combined with other techniques to tackle more difficult problems.

- AHP is easier to understand and can effectively manage both qualitative and quantitative data.

Despite the wide application of AHP in various fields, it has been criticised from several points of view [Lahby 2013] :

- The AHP method requires dependency between elements of the same hierarchical level;
- The decision-maker may find it extremely difficult to express his preferences and provide binary comparative judgements;
- the number of pairwise comparisons increases as the number of criteria or alternatives increases;
- In the majority of situations, the RC coherence ratio exceeds 10%, which means that the comparison matrix has to be reconstructed.

In order to overcome these limitations, the AHP method has been extended in several ways, in particular by taking account of uncertainty in the expression of user judgements (fuzzy AHP).

4.2.2 Fuzzy AHP

Due to the imprecision and uncertainty of user judgements in the binary comparison between criteria and between alternatives, AHP seems insufficient to capture user judgements with better accuracy; for this reason, fuzzy logic [Zadah 1965] was first introduced by [Laarhoven et al., 1983] into the AHP method to overcome this limitation. In fuzzy set theory, a fuzzy set is defined by a membership function and each element has a membership degree. Different types of fuzzy membership functions have been proposed: monotonic, triangular and trapezoidal. According to [Laarhoven et al 1983], [Buckley 1985], [Chang 1996], [Kwong and Bai 2002] and [Tang 2009], triangular fuzzy numbers (TFN) are the most appropriate because of their computational simplicity and they are successfully applied in many applications.

The different stages of the fuzzy AHP method :

- Step1: Structuring the problem as a hierarchy: Similar to AHP, the first step consists of decomposing the complex decision problem into a hierarchical structure.
- Step 2: Elicit the importance of the elements: to indicate the scale of importance of each element, the net values of AHP are replaced by triangular fuzzy numbers (1,3,5,7,9), or :

Table 4. Triangular fuzzy numbers

Net value	Fuzzy number	Function
1	T	(1.1, 2)
3	3	(2,3, 4)
5	5	(4,5, 6)
7	7	(6,7, 8)
9	9	(8, 9,10)

- Step 3: constructing the fuzzy comparison matrix

By means of the fuzzy binary comparison between each two elements, the matrix A is constructed as follows:

$$\tilde{A}=\begin{bmatrix} 1 & \tilde{a}_{12} & \dots & \tilde{a}_{1n} \\ \tilde{a}_{21} & 1 & \dots & \tilde{a}_{2n} \\ & & & \\ \tilde{a}_{n1} & \tilde{a}_{n2} & \dots & 1 \end{bmatrix} \quad (4.9)$$

Or, atjj is a triangular fuzzy number :

$$\tilde{a}_{ij}=\begin{cases} \tilde{1},\tilde{3},\tilde{5},\tilde{7},\tilde{9} \text{ or } \tilde{1}^{-1},\tilde{3}^{-1},\tilde{5}^{-1},\tilde{7}^{-1},\tilde{9}^{-1} & i \neq j \\ 1 & i=j \end{cases}$$

Step4: solve for fuzzy eigenvectors, where $\tilde{\lambda}$ is a fuzzy number, solution a :

$$\tilde{A}\tilde{x}=\tilde{\lambda}\tilde{x} \quad (4.10)$$

Or: A is an n*n matrix, containing the fuzzy numbers $\tilde{a}_{ij}$, $\tilde{x}$ est un n* vector .1

Fuzzy multiplication and addition are performed using arithmetic and a-sliced intervals.

The degree of satisfaction with the judgement matrix $\tilde{A}$ is estimated using the optimism index p. A higher value of the index λ indicates a higher degree of optimism.

A

$$a^{\alpha}_{ij}=\lambda\tilde{a}^{\alpha}_{iju}+(1-\lambda)\tilde{a}^{\alpha}_{ijl},\forall\lambda\in[0,1] \quad (4.11)$$

When a is fixed, the following matrix can be obtained after defining the optimism index λ, in order to estimate the degree of satisfaction.

$$\tilde{A}=\begin{bmatrix} 1 & a_{12} & \dots & a_{1n} \\ a_{21} & 1 & \dots & a_{2n} \\ & & & \\ a_{n1} & a_{n2} & \dots & 1 \end{bmatrix} \quad (4.12)$$

The five triangular fuzzy numbers are defined with the corresponding importance intensity as follows:

$$\begin{aligned} &\tilde{1}_{\alpha}=[1,3-2\alpha] \\ &\tilde{3}_{\alpha}=[1+2\alpha,5-2\alpha],\tilde{3}_{\alpha}^{-1}=[1/(5-2\alpha),1/(1+2\alpha)] \\ &\tilde{5}_{\alpha}=[3+2\alpha,7-2\alpha],\tilde{5}_{\alpha}^{-1}=[1/(7-2\alpha),1/(3+2\alpha)] \\ &\tilde{7}_{\alpha}=[5+2\alpha,9-2\alpha],\tilde{7}_{\alpha}^{-1}=[1/(9-2\alpha),1/(5+2\alpha)] \\ &\tilde{9}_{\alpha}=[7+2\alpha,11-2\alpha],\tilde{9}_{\alpha}^{-1}=[1/(11-2\alpha),1/(7+2\alpha)] \end{aligned} \quad (4.13)$$

- Step 5: check the consistency of the user's judgements: in the same way as the AHP method.
- Step 6: Prioritisation and ranking of alternatives.

4.2.3 Entropy

Shannon entropy [Shannon 1948] is the most popular objective weighting method; it is a measure that uses probability theory to measure the uncertainty of information.

The steps in the entropy method are :

Step 1: calculate the entropy of each criterion as follows:

$$E_j = -k\sum_{i=1}^{m} r_{ij}\, ln(r_{ij}), 1 \le i \le m, 1 \le j \le n. \quad (4.14)$$

Where: m represents the number of alternatives and :

$$k = 1/ln(m). \quad (4.15)$$

$$r_{ij} = a_{ij} / \sum_{i=1}^{n} a_{ij}. \quad (4.16)$$

Step2: calculate the degree of dëviation as follows:

$$d_j = 1 - E_j \quad (4.17)$$

The degree of dëviation shows how useful the erкëre j is to the dëcideur. If there is a small difference between the values of a cтKëre, this means that the alternatives are indifferent according to this crit^re.

Step3: Calculate the entropy weight for each cтKëre :

$$w_j = d_j / \sum_{j=1}^{n} d_j \quad 1 \le j \le n. \quad (4.18)$$

4.3 Storage methods

In this section, we will present the multicriteria decision support methods that have been proposed in the literature for ranking alternatives. Several research projects have exploited these methods for selecting Web services.

These include PROMETHEE [Brans et al, 1985] , ELECTRE [Roy 1968] and TOPSIS [Hwang et al, 1981].

4.3.1 PROMETHEE

The PROMETHEE method (Preference Ranking Organization METHod for Enrichment Evaluations) was proposed by [Brans et al, 1985]; It is an MCDM method which allows a partial or global ranking of alternatives according to their relevance, including the user's preferences (weights, preferences and indifference thresholds), it is an outranking method where each pair of alternatives is compared; it is based on the extension of the notion of cтKëre by the introduction of a preference function. For each criterion, the user is called to choose a preference function among the six proposed functions (Figure. 17), the paramëtres of the functions are represented by the preference and indifference thresholds [Albadvi et al., 2007] [Ayadi 2010].

The steps of the PROMETHEE method are :

- Step : For each criterion, set one of the six basic functions proposed in PROMETHEE (usual criterion, U-shape criterion, V-shape criterion, level criterion, V-shape with indifference criterion and Gaussian criterion).
- Step 2: For each pair of alternatives (a_i, a_k), the degree of preference (outranking degree) is calculated as follows:

$$P(a_i, a_k) = \sum_{j=1}^{n} \pi_j . F_j(a_i, a_k) \quad (4.19)$$

Where π_j represents the weight of criterion number j.

- Step 3: Calculate the positive and negative flows for each alternative:

The positive flow indicates the strength of the alternative *ai*

$$\Phi^{+}(a_i)=\sum_{a_k \neq a_i} P(a_i,a_k) \tag{4.20}$$

The flow пёдайГ indicates the weakness of 1 alternative *ai*

$$\Phi^{-}(a_i)=\sum_{a_k \neq a_i} P(a_k,a_i) \tag{4.21}$$

Step4: PROMETHEE II is used to rank the alternatives according to the net flow score Φ (ai), defined as follows:

$$\Phi(a_i)=\Phi^{+}(a_i)-\Phi^{-}(a_i) \tag{4.22}$$

According to [Rehman et al., 2012], the PROMETHEE method is an improved form of the ELECTRE outranking method, differing in the binary comparison step between alternatives. Whereas ELECTRE determines whether a particular alternative is better than another, through tests of concordance and discordance, the PROMETHEE method considers the degree of preference to determine whether one alternative is preferable to another, this information can be used to eliminate dominated alternatives and identify non-dominated or least dominated alternatives.

PROMETHEE classifies alternatives in a partial or complete way and is easier to use, less complex than the ELECTRE method and offers several very useful preference functions [Peng et al., 2013] .

1ère forme : Vrai-critère 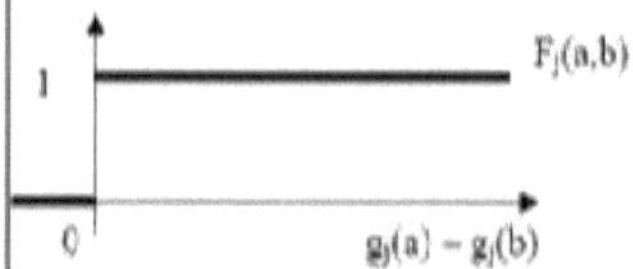	• Préférence stricte immédiate. • Pas de paramètres à déterminer. $F_j(a,b)=\begin{cases}1 & si \quad g_j(a)>g_j(b)\\ 0 & si \quad g_j(a)\leq g_j(b)\end{cases}$
2ème forme : Quasi-critère 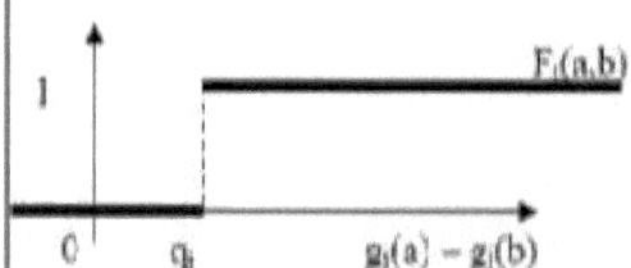	• Il existe un seuil d'indifférence (quasi-critère) qui doit être fixé. $F_j(a,b)=\begin{cases}1 & si \quad g_j(a)-g_j(b)>q_j\\ 0 & si \quad g_j(a)-g_j(b)\leq q_j\end{cases}$
3ème forme : Pré-critère 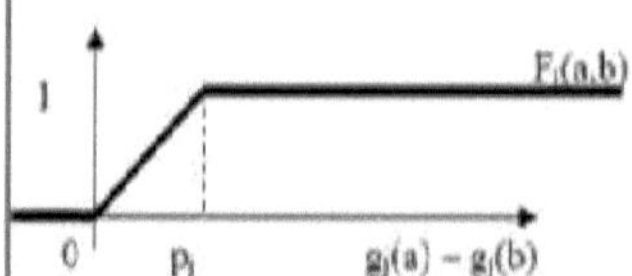	• La préférence croit jusqu'à un seuil de préférence qui doit être fixé. $F_j(a,b)=\begin{cases}1 & si \quad g_j(a)-g_j(b)>p_j\\ \dfrac{g_j(a)-g_j(b)}{p_j} & si \quad 0<g_j(a)-g_j(b)\leq p_j\\ 0 & si \quad g_j(a)-g_j(b)\leq 0\end{cases}$
4ème forme : Pseudo-critère 1 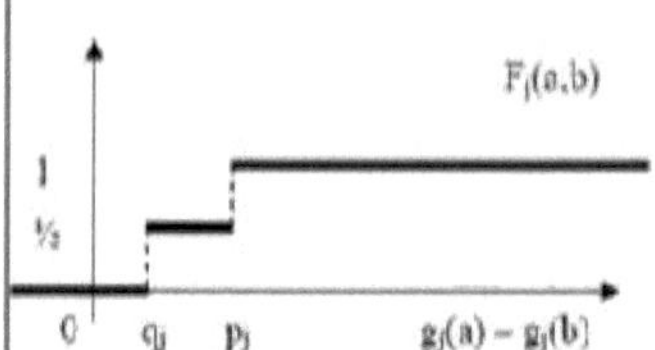	• Il existe un seuil d'indifférence et un seuil de préférence à fixer (pseudo-critère); entre les deux, la préférence est moyenne. $F_j(a,b)=\begin{cases}1 & si \quad g_j(a)-g_j(b)>p_j\\ ½ & si \quad q_j<g_j(a)-g_j(b)\leq p_j\\ 0 & si \quad g_j(a)-g_j(b)\leq q_j\end{cases}$

5ème forme : Pseudo-critère 2 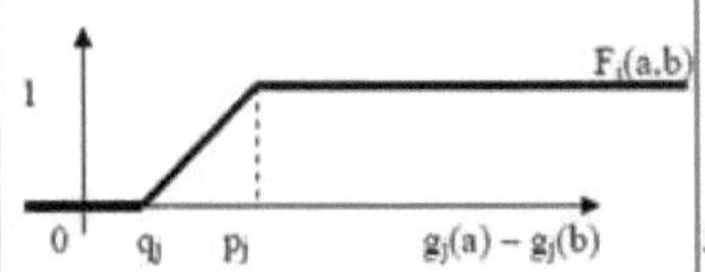	• Il existe un seuil d'indifférence et un seuil de préférence à fixer; entre les deux la préférence est croissante. $F_j(a,b)=\begin{cases} 1 & si\ g_j(a)-g_j(b)>p_j \\ \frac{g_j(a)-g_j(b)-q_j}{p_j-q_j} & si\ q_j<g_j(a)-g_j(b)\leq p_j \\ 0 & si\ g_j(a)-g_j(b)\leq q_j \end{cases}$
6ème forme : Critère gaussien 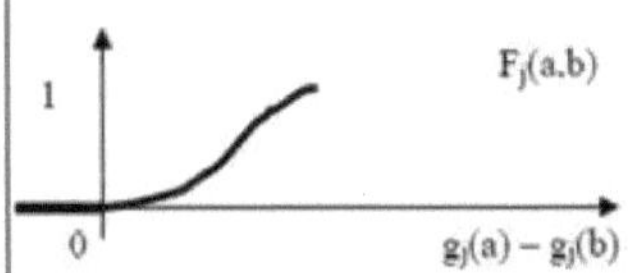	• La préférence croit suivant une loi gaussienne dont il faut fixer l'écart type. $F_j(a,b)=1-\exp(\frac{g_j(a)-g_j(b)}{-2\sigma^2})$ (avec σ = écart-type)

Figure 17. PROMETHEE preference functions [Ayadi 2010] .

4.3.2 ELECTRE

ELECTRE is an MCDM method developed by [Roy 1968], it is a series of so-called outranking methods that were initialized by the same author with his team (ELECTRE I, ELECTRE II, ELECTRE III, ELECTRE IV, ELECTRE IS, and ELECTRE TRI) [Ayadi 2010] [Mohammadshahi et al., 2013]. According to [Whaiduzzaman et al., 2014] the simplest variant of the ELECTRE methods involves up to 10 steps, it performs a binary comparison between alternatives to determine their outranking relationships, these relationships are then exploited to identify and eliminate alternatives that are dominated by others, thus producing a smaller set of alternatives.

The ELECTRE family of methods can be used to solve three types of problem:

- Choice problem: this consists of selecting as small a subset as possible from the set of alternatives, such as ELECTRE I and ELECTRE Is ;
- Sorting problem: this involves assigning each alternative to a predefined class: ELECTRE Sort.
- Ranking problem: this involves ranking the alternatives from best to worst, such as: ELECTRE II, ELECTRE III and ELECTRE IV.

4.3.3 TOPSIS

The TOPSIS method (Technique for Order of Preferences by Similarity to Ideal Solution) was proposed by [Hwang et al., 1981], its principle is to find a solution that is close to the idëal solution, and away from the worst solution. This mëthod shows a prëfërence for similarity to an idëal solution. In this mëthod, the dëcision matrix is first normalisedëe using vector normalisation, and the idëal and anti-idëal solutions are identified in the normalisëe dëcision matrix.

The ëtapes of the TOPSIS mëthod are rësumëes as follows [Lahby 2013]:

- Step 1 : normalising the performance matrix ;
- Step2 : weightërer the normalisëe performance matrix ;
- Step3 : dëterminate the positive idëal solution A+ and the ligtitive idëal solutionA- ;
- Step 4 : calculate the distance between each alternative and A+ and A -;
- Step5 : Calculate the coefficient C, which measures the distance between each

alternative and the
two solutions idëal and ^gative.

- Step 6: Rank the alternatives according to C.

4.4 Selection of Web Services using MCDM methods

The use of imulritated dëcision support mëthods for solving certain problems is not new. In the context of Web services sëlection, several approaches basedë on MCDM mëthods have ëlë proposëes.

- In the work of [Godse et al., 2008], the authors propose an approach based on the AHP method for the sëlection of Web services. The proposed hierarchical structure is composed of three levels, the first level describes the main objective which is the selection of Web services, the second level presents the three factors : service security, service quality and business consent, in the third level, each factor and dëclinë into a set of attributes. The attributes have ëlë weightërës, the prior vectors have ëlë calcutes and the web services have ëlë rankës, allowing the end user to sëlect the most relevant web services.
- [Seo et al.2005] proposes an approach that enables the sëlection of Web services by exploiting the outranking relations of the PROMETHEE mëthod. The authors justify the choice of the PROMETHEE mëthod over the AHP and MAUT mëthods by: o PROMETHEE allows alternatives that are difficult to classify to be ranked by comparing it with other mëthods such as AHP and MAUT.

o PROMETHEE does not require the user to fill in several comparison matrices between alternatives, particularly when deleting or inserting new alternatives, as is the case for the AHP method.

To demonstrate the feasibility of this approach, a case study was carried out on a sample of five Web services. Five service quality criteria were taken into account and the same weight was assigned to the different selection criteria. After calculating the positive, negative and net flows, the Web services were ranked in a complete manner using the net flow.

- [Silas et al., 2012], proposes a Framework for Web Services Selection based on the ELECTRE III method, it consists of four modules: request processing, service selection, job monitoring and service delivery. The Request Processing module allows users to submit requests for the selection of desired services with requirements and preferences for each criterion, it assigns a job for each user request and registers it as a request job. The service selection module evaluates the request, selecting the best service provider according to the user's requirements and preferences. The monitoring module keeps track of execution tasks. The transfer of the service selection result is carried out by the service delivery module, which also provides the service cost.

According to the authors, the selection of relevant services based on user needs is a multi-criteria decision support problem. The values assigned to the preferences of the selection criteria play a very important role in the selection process. In this work, the ELECTRE III multi-criteria decision support method is used to perform a total ranking of services.

- In [Chakhar et al. 2011], the authors define an approach for the selection and composition of Web services based on the ELECTRE TRI method. The objective is to classify Web services into a set of categories in order to optimise their compositions. Three categories have been defined: recommended composition, non-recommended composition and intermediate composition.
- [Karim et al., 2011] proposes an improved version of the PROMETHEE method for the

selection of Web services. The authors use the ANP method to compute the weights of the QoS criteria. During the selection process, the user needs to choose for each QoS criterion a preference function among the six proposed, and for some preference functions it is required to introduce values for prëfërences and indifference thresholds. These paraтёйез offered by PROMETHEE are very important in order to improve the precision and flexibility of the sëlection process. In several cases, when the difference between two alternatives in a стКёге is negligible, 1 user can consider that the two alternatives are equal with respect to this criterion, which is called an indifference relationship. In other cases, when the difference is significant, the user may define it as a preference relationship.

After specifying the preference functions for each стКёге, a binary comparison between two Web services to calculate the differences matrix, then, this matrix is used to calculate the preference intensity between two Web services. The preference intensity takes values between 0 and 1. When its value is equal to 0, it means that the two Web services are indifferent with respect to this criterion; when the value is close to 0, it implies that the preference relationship is weak; on the other hand when the value of the preference intensity is close to 1, the preference relationship is strong.

The preference intensity matrix is used to calculate the degree of preference between each two Web services, this relationship expressing the degree to which a Web service si outranks another Web service Sj; then, the positive, negative and net flows are calculated; PROMETHEE I uses the first two flows (positive and negative) to carry out a partial ranking of the Web services, preserving the indifference and incomparability preference relationships. The net flow is used by PROMETHEE II to carry out a total ranking of the proposed Web services.

The authors propose a new version of PROMETHEE II, integrating into the ordering process a Web service called R that includes the user's QoS requirements; all Web services that outperform the R Web service will be returned to the user.

- In [Nacer et al, 2015], a Web services ranking approach has been proposed, it is based on concordance and discordance tests between QoS crores, this approach is inspired by the ELECTRE method; the strict dominance relation is replaced by an outranking relation; (i) the concordance test uses a majority rule to decide between each two Web services, more precisely, this test represents the strength of the union of QoS criteria that are in favour for one Web service to outrank another, (ii) the discordance test measures the degree to which a QoS стКёге is strongly opposed to the declaration that one Web service outranks another; in other words, the mismatch test introduces a complementary notion to strongly account for minority conflict. To demonstrate the effectiveness of this approach, the authors compared the result with that returned by the Pareto dominance relation.
- In [Vesyropoulos et al., 2014], the authors use a variety of MCDM methods and test their applicability in the domain of web service selection and composition, focusing mainly on e-commerce transaction scenarios; five methods were used namely: Five methods were used: AHP, PROMETHEE, ELECTRE III, NAIADE and MACBETH; the aim was to test the behaviour of these methods in this context and to assess the advantages and disadvantages of applying each method. A case study was carried out on a set of four Web services with five QoS criteria. The authors found that the results of the five MCDM methods converged, indicating the existence of similarities in the way these methods handle data and the type of process that occurs. A comparison between these five methods is presented in the following table:

Table 5. Comparison between the five MCDMs [Vesyropoulos et al., 2014],.

Method	traceability	User-defined weights	Degree of compensation	Inputs/effort required	Handling uncertainty
AHP	High (hierarchical model)	Yes	High	Medium/High	Only in blurred AHP
PROMETHEE	Average	Yes	Average	Average	Yes, indifference / preference thresholds
MACBETH	Average	Yes	Average	Medium/High	Yes
NAIADE	Low	No	Customisable through operators	Low/Medium	Yes
ELECTRE III	Average	Yes	Does not allow compensation	Average	Yes, indifference / preference thresholds

- [Sun et al. 2014] proposes a Framework for the selection of Web services in the context of cloud computing; a fuzzy ontology has been constructed to find similar Web services that satisfy the user's query; the Fuzzy AHP method has been used for the weighting of QoS criteria; the Fuzzy TOPSIS method is exploited for the ranking of Web services. The authors have demonstrated the effectiveness of this approach by comparing it with other approaches.
- In the work proposed by [Serrai et al., 2016], the authors combine the Skyline, BMW and VIKOR methods for the selection of Web services. the same authors [Serrai et al., 2017], used several MCDM methods for the selection of Web services: Skyline to reduce the search space and Eliminate the domino Web services; BMW to weightërer the QoS criteria; SAW, VIKOR, COPRAS, TOPSIS and BORDAS to rank the Web services. The methods used allow greater precision in the selection process and less complexity in the calculation. Each method was tested separately to assess its ability to select the optimal OlOments, then, to find the best compromise between these ranking methods, the BORDA voting method was applied to determine the compromised solution.
- In a very recent study [Kumar et al, 2018], AHP is combined with TOPSIS to rank web services in the cloud according to the following steps: (1) calculation of the relative weights of the different QoS criteria and identification of the decision matrix, (2) normalisation of the decision matrix, (3) construction of the normalised and weighted decision matrix by multiplying each column of the decision matrix by the weights of the associated QoS criteria, (4) identification of ideal and anti-ideal solutions, (5) calculation of distances, (6) calculation of the coefficient of similarity to the ideal solution, (7) ranking of alternatives according to the coefficient of similarity.

A case study was carried out on a sample of three Web services with six QoS criteria; the result was compared with the results returned by the two AHP and fuzzy AHP methods.

4.5 Summary of Web Services Selection Work Based on MCDM Methods

In the following table, we present a comparative study of existing Web service selection approaches based on MCDM methods, taking into account the following criteria:

1- Elimination of dominant Web services ;
2- Use of QoS data to calculate objective weights ;
3- Calculation of subjective weights based on user opinions ;
4- Dealing with uncertainty in user judgements ;
5- Handling uncertainty in QoS data.
6- Consideration of user preferences in the selection process for Skyline Web services.
7- Number of Web services and QoS criteria taken into account in the experimental studies.

Table 6. Comparison of service selection approaches based on MCDM.

Approach	MCDM methods used	Elimination of dominant Web services	Subjective weighting	Ponderati on Objective	Uncertainty in the user's judgements	Uncertainty in QoS data	User preferences	Number of services / number of criteria

[Godse et al. 2008]	AHP	No	AHP	No	No	No	No	3 / 5
[Seo et al. 2005]	PROMETHEE	No	Enter	No	No	Preference function	Preference thresholds	5 / 5
[Chakhar et al. 2011]	ELECTRE TRI	No	Enter	No	No	Preference settings	Preference settings	4 / 3
[Seo et al. 2004]	MAUT	No	Enter	No	No	No	No	5 / 3
[Karim et al. 2011]	ANP-PROMETHEE	No	OTP	No	No	Preference function	Preference thresholds	8 / 9
[Sun et al. 2014]	AHP Floue	No	AHP Floue	No	AHP Floue	No	No	20 / 12
[Rehman et al. 2014]	ELECTRETOPSIS	No	Enter	No	No	No	Preference settings	5 / 4
[Ouadah et al. 2015a]	Skyline-AHP-PROMETHEE	Skyline	AHP	No	No	No	Preference thresholds	2507/8
[Ouadah et al. 2015b]	Skyline-AHP-PROMETHEE	Skyline	AHP	No	No	No	Preference thresholds	2507/8 21961 / 10
[Alam et al. 2016]	AHP Floue- Fuzzy VIKOR- Fuzzy TOPSIS	No	AHP Floue	No	AHP Floue	Fuzzy VIKOR-Fuzzy TOPSIS	No	-
[Lin et al. 2016]	DEMATEL- PCA-ANP- VICTOR	No	OTP	No	No	No	No	6 / 7
[Serrai et al. 2016]	Skyline-BWM-VIKOR	Skyline	BWM	No	No	No	No	100 / 5
[Sun et al. 2016]	Entropy- TOPSIS	No	No	Entropy	No	No	No	12 / 6
[Kumar et al. 2017]	AHP- Fuzzy TOPSIS	No	AHP	No	No	Fuzzy TOPSIS	No	6 / 10
[Serrai et al. 2017]	Skyline-BWM, SAW, VIKOR, COPRAS, TOPSIS	Skyline	BWM	No	No	No	No	2507/8
[Kumar et al. 2018]	AHP-TOPSIS	No	AHP	No	No	No	No	3 / 6
[Ouadah et al. 2018]	Skyline- Entropy-AHP Floue-PROMETHEE	Skyline	AHP Floue	Entropy	AHP Floue	Preference function	Preference thresholds	2507/8 21961 / 10

In Table 6, we present a comparative study of approaches based on multi-criteria decision support methods (MCDMs) for the selection of Web services. Several methods have been used: AHP [Godse et al., 2008] is used both to weight QoS criteria and to rank Web services. However, when the number of services becomes large, it will be very difficult or even impossible in some cases to fill in several comparison matrices between Web services for each QoS criterion; PROMETHEE [Heressen et al. 2008] requires several user inputs such as the weights of the QoS criteria which are not computed by the PROMETHEE mëthode itself, forcing the end user to assign them manually or use another weighting mëthode such as AHP [Karim et al., 2011]; ELECTRE Tri [Chakhar et al., 2011] performs a classification of Web services into a set of categories in order to optimise their compositions;

We have observed that almost all of the work proposed has been validated on sets of donees where the number of Web services and the number of QoS criteria are very small (see Table 6, column: number of services / criteria). However the number of services published on the Web increases daily, therefore these approaches require a lot of computation time to find the most relevant Web services. Also, using some mëthods like AHP, PROMETHEE or ELECTRE for Web services ranking iK'cess a lot of computation time because of the very large number of binary comparisons between candidate Web services. However, reducing the number of candidates by ëcarting irrelevant Web services reduces the number of comparisons and therefore considerably improves the performance of approaches based on these mëthods.

Other ëstudies have proposedë approaches where several mëthods have ëlë combined in order to overcome the drawbacks present by some of them and exploit the advantages of each mëthod; [Sun et al. 2014] proposes a Framework appuyë on the combination between AHP to assign weights to QoS criteria and Fuzzy TOPSIS to rank its cloud Web services; [Kumar et al., 2018] combines AHP with TOPSIS for ranking Web services in the context of cloud computing. [Serrai et al. 2017] proposes to combine several mëthods: Skyline to reduce the search space, BWM to weight QoS criteria, SAW, VIKOR, COPRAS and TOPSIS to perform Web services ranking. These approaches are basedëes on mëthodes that allow more precision in the sëlection process and less complexity^ in the computation. However, they do not allow the uncertainty in the QoS data and in the user preferences to be taken into account in the selection process. On the other hand, there are approaches that only exploit QoS donees to weightërer QoS criteria [Sun et al. 2016] without taking into account user prëfërences.

4.6 Conclusion

In this chapter, we have corrrencë by presenting a ëtat de l'art on multi-criteria dëcision support methods (MCDMs), then, we have c^ë the research works that exploit these mëthods to weightërer QoS criteria or sëlect the most relevant Web services that meet user prëfërences. At the end of this chapter, we prësentë a ëcomparative study between these approaches, relying on a number of criteria.

Several approaches have been proposed in the literature for the selection of Web services. These approaches are based on multi-criteria decision support methods (MCDM) such as AHP, PROMETHEE, ELECTRE and TOPSIS. We have observed that most of this work has been validated on data sets where the number of Web services is very small, although the number of services published on the Web is increasing daily.

Some approaches have proposedë to combine several mëthods within a single approach in order to overcome the inconvënients prësentës by some of them and to exploit the advantages of each mëthod.

In the next chapter we will present our three approaches SkyAP-S3, SEFAP and IFAHP for the sëlection of Web services.

Part II

Contributions

5 Contributions

5.1 Introduction

In this thesis, we propose three approaches: the SkyAP-S3 approach is a hybrid approach based on the combination of several multicriteria decision support methods (MCDM), namely: the Skyline to reduce the search space, AHP to weight the QoS criteria, and PROMETHEE to capture the user's preferences and rank the Skyline Web services. The SEFAP approach, an improved version of SkyAP-S3, involves dealing with uncertainty in user judgements when weighting QoS criteria. The IFAHP approach is an improved version of the Fuzzy AHP method, for ranking Skyline Web services. In this new version, the comparison matrices between the QoS criteria and between the representative Skyline Web services will be generated automatically by exploiting a discretisation algorithm on the QoS data.

5.2 SkyAP-S3: Hybrid approach

The first approach proposed is the SkyAP-S3 approach (Skyline Ahp Promethee for Skyline Services Selection), which is based on a combination of three multi-criteria decision support methods: Skyline, AHP and PROMETHEE (see Figure 18).

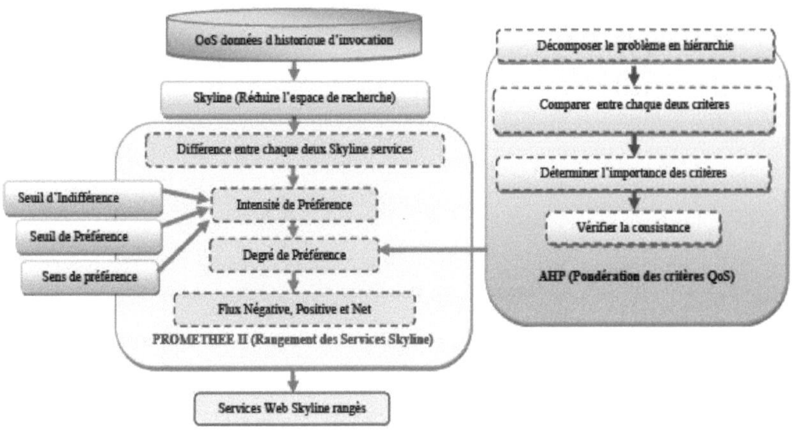

Figure 18. The SkyAP-S3 approach

In the first ëstage of this approach we use the Skyline operator to rOduce the search space and focus only on the set of services that are not dominated by any other service. The BNL algorithm is ийНзё to compute the Skyline result due to its simplicityO and wide usage [Borzsonyi et al., 2001]. To improve the performance of this approach, we propose that this firstëre Otape should be executed offline, before the user's query is received, which will save the Skyline computation time. If a new service is inserted or the QoS of an existing service is modified, the Skyline result is recalculated offline.

In the second step of this approach, we use the AHP method to weight the QoS criteria. The choice of the AHP method [Saaty 1987] is based on the following criteria:

1- AHP is based on a binary comparison between criteria using linguistic terms (low importance, important, etc.), which are easy for users to use to explain their preferences in relation to QoS criteria.

2- AHP allows you to vërify the cohërence of the user's preferences by pressing the two indicators: cohOrence indicator (CI) and cohOrence ratio (CR).

The final step is to apply the PROMETHEE II method to the ranking of Skyline Web services, offering the user an ordered short list of Skyline Web services that have a good compromise between the criteria and that best meet the user's preferences. To make user preferences explicit, we use the V-shape No. 5 preference function, with both preference and indifference thresholds.

$$F_j(S_i,S_k)=\begin{cases}1 & \text{if } G_j(S_i)-G_j(S_k)>p_j\\ \dfrac{G_j(S_i)-G_j(S_k)-q_j}{p_j-q_j} & \text{if } q_j<G_j(S_i)-G_j(S_k)\leq p_j\\ 0 & \text{if } G_j(S_i)-G_j(S_k)\leq q_j\end{cases} \quad (5.1)$$

Where: *pj* represents the preference threshold; qj represents the indifference threshold;

Fj(Si ,Sk) : The intensity of preference between the two services *Si* and *Sk*

Gj*(Si)* : The value of Web service i with respect to QoS criterion j.

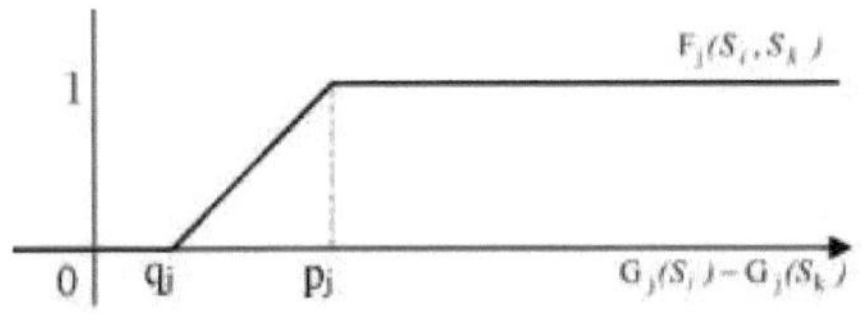

Figure 19. Promethee's V-shape N°5 preference function.

This function allows the user to express his preferences for each QoS criterion, and accepts the following parameters:

- the preference threshold p_i :
- the indifference threshold q_i and
- the direction of preference: whether the QoS criterion is to be minimised, such as *response time*, or maximised, such as *availability*.

In this stage, Skyline Web Services will be ranked using outranking relationships, exploiting the preferences expressed by the user on QoS criteria.

5.2.1 Ranking algorithm

The following algorithm implements the various stages of the PROMETHEE method for ranking Skyline Web services. It starts by calculating the preference intensity between two Skyline Web services, then determines the degree of preference between the two services. Finally, it calculates the three flows: positive, negative and net. The Net flow is used to rank Skyline web services.

- The lines of code between 8 and 31 calculate the intensity of preference between each two Skyline Web Services for each criterion.
- The lines of code between 33 and 42 calculate the degree of preference between the two Skyline web services.
- The lines of code between 44 and 53 calculate the negative flow, which expresses the weakness of the Skyline web service, the positive flow, which determines the strength of the Skyline web service, and the net flow. Finally, the Skyline Web services are ranked according to the net flow.

Algorithm 5.1: Storing Skyline Web services

Algorithme 5.1 : Rangement des services Web Skyline

```
Input:   Skyline services (services Web incomparable) Gj (Si)
Input:   Seuils de préférences Pref [QoSi]
Input:   Seuils d'indifference Indef [QoSi].
Input:   Sens de préférence :  Sense [QoSi].
Input:   Poids des critères of QoS: Weight [QoSi], résultat de AHP
output   Rangement des services Web Skyline
         //Calcul de l'intensité de préférence : n : nombre de services Web, m : nombre de critères
         For I = 1 to n do
          For k = 1 to  n do
             For j =  1 to m do
                Diffj [Sk, Sj] = Gj (Si) – Gj [Sk];
                 If Diffj [Si, Sk] <0 and Sense [QoSi] = min then
                   If Indef [QoSi] < ABS (Diff [QoSi]) <= Pref [QoSi] then
           Fj (Si, Sk) = (ABS (Diffj [Sk, Sj]- Indef [QoSi]) / (Pref [QoSi] – Indef [QoSi]) ;
                       else
                 If ABS (Diffj [Sk, Sj]))> Pref [QoSi] then
                   Fj (Si, Sk) = 1
                 else
                   Fj (Si, Sk) = 0
               else
                If Diffj [Sk, Sj]>0 and Sense [QoSi] = max then
                 If Indef [QoSi] <= Diffj [Sk, Sj] <= Pref [QoSi] then
                Fj (Si, Sk) = (Diffj [Sk, Sj]- Indef [QoSi]) / (Pref [QoSi] – Indef [QoSi]) ;
                 else
                   If Indef [QoSi] > Diffj [Sk, Sj] then
                     Fj (Si, Sk) = 0 ;
                    else
                     Fj (Si, Sk) = 1 ;
             end for
           end for
         end for
         //Calcul de degré de préférence :
         For i =  1 to  n do
            For k = 1 to  n do
               nap = 0;
               For j =1 to  m do
                  If  Si <> Sk then
                   nap = nap + Fj (Si, Sk) * Weight [QoSj];
               end for
                  P (Si, Sk) = nap;
              end for
           end for
         //Calcul du flux Positif, Négatif et Net
         For i = 1 to n do
               temp1 = 0, temp2 = 0
                For j going of 1 in n do
                 temp1 = temp1 + P (Si, Sj) ;
                 temp2 = temp2 + P (Si, Sj);
                end for
                Phpositive (Sj) = temp1;
                Phnegative (Sj) = temp2;
                Phnet (Sj) = temp1 – temp2;
           end for
         Rangement des services Web Skyline selon Phnet.
```

5.2.2 Case study

We present a ëcase study to illustrate the different ëstages of our approach, exploiting QoS data from the QWS DataSet database[9] [Al-Masri et al., 2007a].

Table 7. Examples of QoS data.

Service	Name	Response time (ms)	Debit	Reliability	Best practice	Documentation	Class	Is Skyline
If	FastWeather	125.44	13.5	86.4	80	91	4	Y
S2	dotsfastweather	129.67	13.2	84.1	80	90	4	N
S3	WeatherForecast	261	1.8	58.1	80	94	3	Y
S4	WeatherFetcher	160	2.2	73.3	84	32	3	Y
S5	WeatherService	190.5	12.4	54	80	8	2	N
S6	GlobalWeather	1463.5	2.4	53.5	84	42	2	Y
S7	ndfdXML	409.33	1.8	41.4	72	96	1	Y

The Web services in Table 7 offer the same functionality for consulting meteorological data, but with different QoS values. They accept two parameters as input: *the pay* and *the city*, and

9 http://www.uoguelph.ca/~qmahmoud/qws/index.html, last accessed on 12 March 2018.

return a set of meteorological information in response, such as: *temperature*, *wind speed*, *visibility*, *meteorological conditions*, etc.

5.2.2.1 Calculating the Skyline result

In this demonstrative example, the two Services s_2 and s_5 are not in the Skyline result, because, s_2 is dominated by s_1 and s_5 is dominated by s_1 too. The five Web Services (s_1, s_3, s_4, s_6 and s_7) are the only Skyline Web Services because they are not dominated by any other service, they are incomparable to each other. The "*Is Skyline*" column in Table 7 indicates whether a Web service is a Skyline Web service.

5.2.2.2 Weighting of QoS criteria

The first step in the AHP method is to decompose the problem into a hierarchy. In this example, the problem selects Skyline Web Services at the top of the hierarchy, while the set of QoS criteria: *response time*, *throughput*, *reliability*, *best practice*, *documentation* and *class*, are positioned at the middle level. The last level contains the candidate Skyline Web Services (s_1, s_3, s_4, s_6 and s_7).

To weight the QoS criteria, a comparison is made between each two criteria, using the Saaty scale (1-9),

Table 8. Calculation of QoS criteria weights.

	Response time	flow	reliability	good practice	documentation	Class	Weight
Response time	1	3	2	4	5	3	**0,35**
flow	1/3	1	1/2	3	4	1/2	**0,14**
reliability	1/2	2	1	4	6	3	**0,26**
Best practice	1/4	1/3	1/4	1	2	1/2	**0,07**
Documentation	1/5	1/4	1/6	1/2	1	1/2	**0,05**
Class	1/3	2	1/3	2	2	1	**0,13**

The consistency test is illustrated as follows:

$\lambda_{max} = (6{,}37 + 6{,}20 + 6{,}35 + 6{,}15 + 6{,}19 + 6{,}41)/6 = 6{,}28.$

Calculate the coherence indicator (*CI)*:

$IC = (\lambda_{max}-1) / (N-1) = (6{,}28-1) / (6-1) = 0{,}06$

Calculate the Cohdence Ratio :

$RC = (IC / ACI) = 100 * (0.06 / 1.24) = 0.04.$

The coherence ratio is *0.04,* which is less than *0.1*, meaning that the weights allocated to the QoS criteria are consistent, and the user's judgements are coherent. The QoS criteria weights will be used in the next stage of Skyline Web Services ranking.

5.2.2.3 Storing Skyline Web Services

1. Choice of preference function

The PROMETHEE method is based on the extension of the criterion concept by the introduction of the preference function for an alternative a_i *with* respect to another alternative a_j. Six types of function have been proposed [Brans et al., 1986], and the user is asked to choose a preference function for each criterion. In our case, we have chosen preference function N°5, the parameters of the function (preference threshold and indifference threshold) must be set by the user. In this example, we use the values in the following table:

Table 9. Preference parameters.

Criteria	Response time	Debit	Reliability	Best practice	Documentation	Class
Preference threshold	5	3	4	6	4	1
Indifference threshold	0,5	0,5	0,4	1	0,5	0,2
Direction of preference	min	max	max	max	max	max

The "*direction of preference*" parameter is used to determine whether the QoS criterion should be minimised or maximised. In this example, the *response time* parameter is to be minimised, while all the other criteria (*throughput, reliability, good practice, documentation* and *class*) are to be maximised.

2. Calculating preference intensity

We use preference function No. 5 (Figure 19, expression *(5.1)*) to calculate the preference intensity between each of the two Skyline Web services. For example, for the *response time* criterion, the preference intensity between the two services s_6 and s_7 is calculated as follows:

$G_i(S_6) - G_i(s_7) = 1463.5 - 409.33 = 1,054.170.$

The "*response time*" criterion should be minimised, so :

$G1\ (s_6) - G1\ (s_7) > p1$ *therefore :* $F1\ (s_6, s_7) = 0.000.$

The preference intensity is calculated between the two Skyline web services s_6 and s_7 for each QoS criterion.

3. Calculating the degree of preference (degree of upgrade)

In this step, the degree of preference between each of the two Skyline Web services is calculated. For example, for the degree of preference between $s_6, S7$:

$$P_i(S_6, S_7) = \sum W_i * F_i(S_6, S_7) = 0,35*0 + 0,14*0,172 + 0,26*1 + 0,07*1 + 0,05*0 + 0,13*0 = 0,354.$$

Table 10. Calculation of the degree of out-ranking between Skyline web services.

	S1	S3	S4	S6	S7	ϕ +	ϕ = ϕ+ - ϕ -
s1		0,490	0,750	0,750	0,820	2,810	2,726
s3	0,014		0,260	0,610	0,680	1,564	0,615
s4	0,035	0,392		0,610	0,694	1,739	0,724
s6	0,035	0,048	0,005		0,354	0,453	-1,867
s7	0,000	0,000	0,000	0,350		0,350	-2,199
ϕ -	0,084	0,949	1,015	2,320	2,549		

4. Calculation of positive, negative and net flows

In this step, the positive flow (Φ^+), the negative flow (Φ) and the Net flow (Φ) are calculated for each Skyline Web service, using expressions *(4.19)*, *(4.20)* and *(4.21)*.

Ranking services according to Net flow gives a complete ranking of Web Skyline services from best to worst as follows (see Table 11):

Table 11.Arrangement of Skyline web services.

Rank	Service	Net Flow
1st	S1	2,726
2nd	S4	0,724
3rd	S3	0,615
4th	S6	-1,867
5th	S7	-2,199

5.3 SEFAP approach

5.3.1 Principle of the approach

The second approach proposed is the SEFAP approach (Skyline, Entropy, Fuzzy Ahp and Prometee), this approach includes the same ëtapes as the SkyAP-S3 approach, except for the weightëration step of the QoS criteria, where AHP has been replaced by Entropy and Fuzzy AHP.

The importance of QoS criteria is a decisive factor in the selection process of Web services, it differs from one context to another and from one user to another, for example, in the context of e-payment, the *security* criterion is more important than the other criteria, but in the context of information retrieval, *response time* and *availability* represent the most important criteria [Ouadah et al., 2018a]. Several techniques have been proposed in the literature to weigh QoS criteria, they are classified into three categories: objective, subjective and hybrid.

1. Objective methods extract weights for QoS criteria from data such as Entorpie [Sun et al., 2016] and FDCW [Almulla et al., 2011].

The major drawback of objective methods is that they do not take into account the opinions of domain experts when calculating weights, relying solely on data that is generally collected automatically over well-defined periods in specific contexts.

2. Subjective methods exploit users' opinions to calculate the weights of QoS criteria: ANP [Karim et al., 2011], AHP [Godse et al., 2008] [Ouadah et al., 2015a, b], Fuzzy AHP [Sun et al., 2014]. However, subjective methods reflect users' subjective judgements which can be vague, imprecise and user-influenced.

3. Hybrid methods combine objective and subjective methods to determine weights by exploiting both QoS data and user opinions [Xiong et al., 2007] [Ma et al., 2013] [Almulla et al., 2015].

In the Skyline SkyAP-S3 Web services selection approach [Ouadah et al., 2015a, b] proposed in the previous chapter, the AHP method is used to weight the QoS criteria, however, this method has certain drawbacks, in particular: the subjectivity and imprecision of users' opinions when filling in several comparison matrices between criteria. In the SEFAP approach, we propose to use a hybrid method composed of Entropy and Fuzzy AHP methods in the QoS criteria weighting phase.

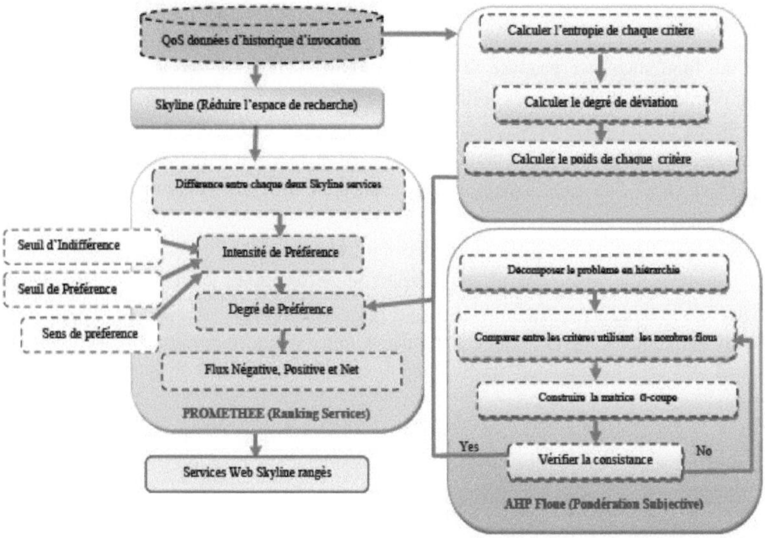

Figure 20. The SEFAP approach.

In the SEFAP approach (Skyline, Entropy, Fuzzy Ahp and Prometee) we propose to

Combining four multi-criteria dëcision support methods for web service ranking. SEFAP allows the advantages of each mëthod to be exploited in order to achieve better performance compared to using each mëthod sëparëment.

1- In the firstëre step of SEFAP, we use the Skyline method to reduce the search space by focusing only on relevant Web services that are not dominated by any other service. By reducing the search space, this will reduce the time taken to rank relevant services, and significantly improve the performance of the approach. As proposed by [Elarifai et al., 2010], this step can be carried out offline in order to improve the performance of the approach; if a new service is added, the Skyline result is recalculated.

2- To weight the QoS criteria, we combine the objective Entropy method with the subjective Fuzzy AHP method. The choice of these methods is justified by the fact that :

- The Entropy method is used to determine the weights of QoS criteria, by exploiting data from the history of invocations made by other users. This is the most widely used method for calculating objective criterion weights.
- Fuzzy AHP exploits the user's opinions and deals with the imprecision and uncertainty in the user's judgements using the fuzzy set theory.
- Fuzzy AHP is based on a binary comparison between each two QoS criteria, relying on linguistic terms (low importance, high importance, ... etc.), which is easier for the user to use. To indicate the scale of importance of the criteria, crisp values are replaced by fuzzy triangular numbers.
- AHP Flou can be used to check the consistency and coherence of the user's opinions by means of a consistency indicator (CI) and a coherence ratio (CR).
- To integrate the objective weights (Wo) and the subjective weights, we assume that the importance of the objective weight is λ, and the importance of the subjective weight is $(1-\lambda)$. . The final weight is therefore calculated as follows:

$$W_j = Wo_j * \lambda + Ws_j * (1-\lambda) \quad (5.1)$$

3- In the final stage, we propose to use the PROMETHEE method to perform a complete ranking of Skyline Web services, offering the user a short list of Skyline Web services that have a better compromise between QoS criteria and that best meet the user's requirements. The choice of the PROMETHEE method is justified by the following reasons:

- PROMETHEE is a simple methodology compared with other outranking methods [Brans et al., 1986];
- It is frequently used in multi-criteria decision support [Behzadian et al., 2010];
- It facilitates the treatment of imprecision in performance data values [Vincke 1992] [Kangas et al. 2001] [Hyde et al. 2003] [Roy et al. 2014] [Balali et al. 2014].
- With the proposed preference functions, it allows the integration of user preferences expressed as a set of parameters (preference threshold, indifference threshold and preference direction) [Brans et al., 2005].

5.3.2 Weighting algorithm for QoS criteria

```
    Algorithme 5.2 : Pondération des critères de QoS
1 : Input :   Comparaison en les critères QoS : Crisp[QoSi, Valj]
2 : Input :   l'index d'optimum λ
3 : Input :   le niveau de confidence α
4 : Output    Poids des critères QoS : Weights[QoSi]
5 :           //Fuzzification en utilisant les nombres flous triangulaires
6 :             For i = 2 to n do
7 :               For j = 1 to n do
8 :                 If Crisp[QoSi, Valj] = 1 then
9                     TFN[i,j,1]:= 1; TFN[i,j,2]:= 3-2 α
10            else If Crisp[QoSi, Valj] = 3 then
11                      TFN[i,j,1]:= 1+2 α; TFN[i,j,2]:= 5-2 α
12            else If Crisp[QoSi, Valj] = 5 then
13                      TFN[i,j,1]:= 3+2 α; TFN[i,j,2]:= 7-2 α
14                  .................................
15              End for
16            end for
17          // Calcul de alpha-coupe et defuzzification
18          For i = 2 to n do
19            For j = 1 to n do
20              Alpha-Cut[i,j]:= TFN[i,j,1] λ + (1- λ) TFN[i,j,2];
21          end for
22          end for
23          For i = 1 to n do
24            Somme :=0;
25              For j = 1 to n do
26            Somme := Somme + Alpha-Cut[j,i];
27                end for
28                  S[i]:= Somme ;
29            End for
30          // Calcul des poids des criteres de QoS :
31          For i = 1 to n do
32            Temp := 0;
33            For j = 1 to n do
34            Temp:= Temp + Alpha-Cut[j,i]/ S[i];
35              end for
36                Weights [QoSi]:= Temp / n ;
37            End for
```

The above algorithm dëcrit les différentes ëtapes pour pondërer les critères de QoS, les lignes de code entre 6 et 16 convert les données de QoS nettes en données floues, les lignes de code entre 17 et 29 calculent alpha coupe, les lignes de code entre 30 et 37 calculent les poids criteria.

5.3.3 Case studies

We will illustrate the various stages of our approach in a case study, using QoS data from the QWS DataSet database[10] [Al-Masri et al., 2007a].

Table 12. Examples of QoS data.

Service	Name	Response time (ms)	Debit	Reliability	Best practice	Documentation	Class	Is Skyline
If	FastWeather	125.44	13.5	86.4	80	91	4	Y
S2	dotsfastweather	129.67	13.2	84.1	80	90	4	N
S3	WeatherForecast	261	1.8	58.1	80	94	3	Y
S4	WeatherFetcher	160	2.2	73.3	84	32	3	Y
S5	WeatherService	190.5	12.4	54	80	8	2	N
S6	GlobalWeather	1463.5	2.4	53.5	84	42	2	Y
S7	ndfdXML	409.33	1.8	41.4	72	96	1	Y

The Web services in Table 12 offer the same functionality for consulting meteorological data with different QoS values. They accept as input the two parameters *pay* and *city*, and return in

[10] http://www.uoguelph.ca/~qmahmoud/qws/index.html, last accessed on 12 March 2018.

response a set of meteorological information such as: temperature, wind speed, visibility, meteorological conditions, etc.

5.3.3.1 Calculating the Skyline result

In this example, the two Services s_2 and s_5 are not in the Skyline result, because s_2 is dominated by s_1 and s_5 is dominated by s_1 too. The five Web services (s_1, s_3, s_4, s_6 and s_7) are the only Skyline Web services, because they are not dominated by any other service, and are incomparable with each other. The "*Is Skyline*" column in Table 7 indicates whether a Web service is a Skyline Web service.

Both Entropy and Fuzzy AHP were used to weight QoS criteria by exploiting both QoS data and user opinions.

5.3.3.2 Objective and subjective weighting

5.3.3.2.1 Calculating target weights

The calculation of objective weights for QoS criteria is based on the Entropy method, which uses the data presented in Table 13:

Table 13. Calculation of Rij.

Response time (ms)	Debit	Reliability	Best practice	Documentation	Class
0,056	0,285	0,180	0,143	0,201	0,211
0,058	0,279	0,175	0,143	0,199	0,211
0,117	0,038	0,182	0,143	0,208	0,158
0,072	0,047	0,153	0,150	0,071	0,158
0,086	0,262	0,113	0,143	0,018	0,105
0,426	0,051	0,112	0,150	0,093	0,105
0,184	0,038	0,086	0,129	0,212	0,053

By applying the different formulas of the Entropy method, Table 14 shows the

result of the calculation of the entropy, the deviation and the weight of each criterion.

Table 14. Calculation of objective weights.

Criteria	Response time (ms)	Debit	Reliability	Best practice	Documentation	Class
Entropy	0,85	0,83	0,98	1,00	0,91	0,96
Deviation	0,15	0,17	0,02	0,00	0,09	0,04
Weight	0,32	0,37	0,04	0,00	0,18	0,09

5.3.3.2.2 Calculating subjective weights

In the first stage of the Fuzzy AHP method, the problem is presented in hierarchical form. In our case, the problem of selecting Skyline Web services is in the first level, in the second level, we find the QoS criteria which are: *response time, throughput, reliability, good practice, documentation* and *class*. The alternatives or Skylie Web services (s_1, s_3, s_4, s_6 and s_7) are at the last level. In the second step, we use Triangular Fuzzy Numbers (TNF) to compare the two criteria and fill in the comparison matrix as follows:

Table 15. Comparison in fuzzy triangular numbers between QoS criteria.

	Response time (ms)	Debit	Reliability	Best practice	Documentation	Class
Response time (ms)	1	3	3	5	9	7
Debit	~-1 3	1	1	3	7	5
Reliability	^"1 3	1	1	3	5	7
Best practice	-1 5	~-1 3	~-1 3	1	5	3
Documentation	-i 9	-1 7	~-1 5	JI/-1 5	1	~-1 3
Class	-1 7	~-1 5	JI/-1 3	""-I 3	3	1

The alpha-cut matrix is calculated using the equations described in section 4.2.2. We have assigned a value of *0.5* to the confidence level (a) and the optimum index (X).

Table 16. The alpha-cut matrix and subjective weights of QoS criteria.

	Response time (ms)	Debit	Reliability	Best practice	Documentation	Class	Weight
Response time (ms)	1,000	3,000	3,000	5,000	9,000	7,000	**0,400**
Debit	0,375	1,000	1,500	3,000	7,000	5,000	**0,208**
Reliability	0,375	1,500	1,000	3,000	5,000	7,000	**0,212**
Best practice	0,208	0,375	0,375	1,000	5,000	3,000	**0,098**
Documentation	0,113	0,146	0,208	0,208	1,000	0,375	**0,029**
Class	0,146	0,146	0,375	0,375	3,000	1,000	**0,053**

The consistency test is illustrated as follows:

$\lambda_{max} = (6,95 + 6,90 + 7,00 + 6,15 + 6,54 + 6,45)/6 = 6,74.$

Calculate the coherence indicator (*CI)*:

$IC = (\lambda_{max}-N) / (N-1) = (6,74-6) / (6-1) = 0,12$

Calculate the coherence ratio :

$RC = IC / ACI = 0.12 / 1.24 = 0.09.$

The consistency ratio is equal to *0.09*. It is less than a *0.1*, which means that the weights allocated to the QoS criteria are consistent, and the user's judgements are coherent. Nevertheless, we find that the consistency ratio obtained with the AHP method (RC= 0.04) is better than that obtained with Fuzzy AHP (RC=0.09). This difference is explained by the fact that AHP Fuzzy uses fuzzy numbers in the comparisons between criteria [Wang et al., 2008] [Liu et al., 2017]. For the AHP method, consistency is guaranteed as long as the transitivity relations are satisfied in the judgements expressed in net values by the user [Zhu 2014].

The subjective weights of the QoS criteria will be combined with the objective weights to calculate hybrid weights, which will be used in the next stage of Skyline web services ranking.

5.3.3.2.3 Calculating hybrid weights

Hybrid weights are calculated by aggregating subjective weights extracted from user opinions with objective weights calculated on the basis of QoS history data. This aggregation makes it possible to incorporate the user's preferences into the selection process and to deal with imprecision in its preferences.

Hybrid weights are calculated using expression (5.1).

By assigning the value 0 to λ , the weights will be reduced to subjective weights only, while assigning the value 1 to 1 will reduce the weights to objective weights only. In this example the value 0.5 is assigned to 1.

$Wj = Woj * 0.5 + Wsj * 0.5$

Table 17. Calculation of hybrid weights.

Criteria	Response time (ms)	Debit	Reliability	Best practice	Documentation	Class
Subjective weights	0,08	0,06	0,08	0,41	0,06	0,30
Target weights	0,40	0.21	0,21	0,1	0,03	0,05
Hybrid weights	0,28	0,135	0,15	0,255	0,045	0,175

5.3.3.3 Partial storage with PROMETHEE I

After calculating the preference intensity, preference degree, positive flow (Φ^+) and negative flow (Φ^-) for each Skyline web service, using expressions (4.19), (4.20) and (4.21), the positive and negative flows can be used to perform a partial ranking of Skyline web services.

Table 18. Calculation of positive, negative and net flows.

Rank	Sn	Service	Positive flow	Negative flow	Net flow
1st	s1	FastWeather	3,166	0,112	3,054
2nd	s4	WeatherFetcher	1,820	1,032	0,788
3rd	s3	WeatherForecast	1,548	1,118	0,331
4th	s6	GlobalWeather	0,431	2,444	-2,013
5th	s7	ndfdXML	0,400	2,660	-2,260

The *FastWeather* service is identified as the best Skyline Web service, with partial rankings as follows: s1, s4, s3, S6 and s7. The two services S6 and S7 are incomparable.

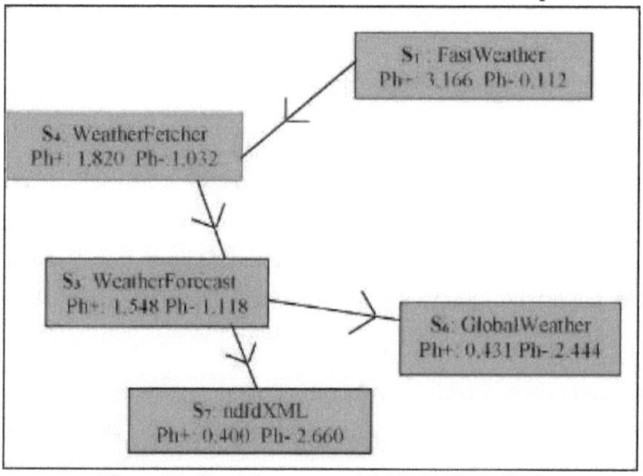

Figure 21. Partial storage with PROMETHEE I

5.3.3.4 Gaia Plan

Gaia's design is an analytical tool [Brans et al 1994] [Albadvi et al 2007], it is ий^ё to extract some observations about alternatives and criteria such as: alternatives that are good on some criteria and bad on others, similar, opposës or indëpendent criteria.

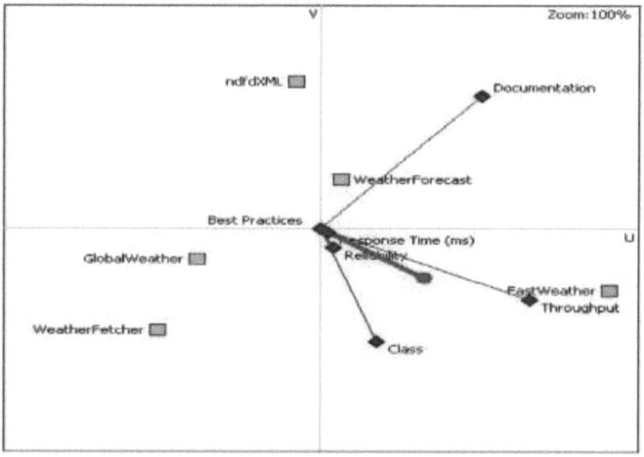

Figure 22. The Gaia plan for the sëlection of Skyline web services.

The Gaia plan relating to the sëlection of the mëtëorological Web services of Skyline is illustrated in Figure 22. Web services are represented by green rectangles and SQ criteria. by blue vectors. The *FastWeather* service is better on *speed,* class and *response time*, but worse on documentation. The two Web services Skyline *ndfdXML* and *WeatherForecast* are good on *documentation* and bad on the other criteria. The criteria (*throughput, response time, reliability, class*) are similar; the criteria (*class and documentation*) are indëpendent. Figure 22 also shows the direction of the accuracy axis (which is represented by the red vector) towards the Skyline *FastWeather* web service, which represents the most relevant meteorological Skyline web service.

5.3.3.5 Sensitivity analysis to changes in QoS criterion weights

The sensitivity analysis given in table 19 provides, for each QoS criterion, the limits in the weights that can be modified without changing the order of the Weather Skyline web service.

Table 19. Sensitivity analysis.

QoS criteria	Response time	Debit	Accessibility	Good practice	Documentation.	Class
Weight	0,280	0,135	0,150	0,255	0,045	0,175
Min	0,000	0,000	0,000	0,000	0,000	0,059
Max	4,435	infinite	97,203	infinite	0,128	infinite

We can see that the *response time, accessibility* and *documentation* criteria have a greater impact on the ranking result for the Skyline meteorologique web service.

5.4 IFAHP approach

The third approach proposëe in our contribution is 1 IFAHP approach [Ouadah et al., 2018d]. It is a атëHorëe version of fuzzy AHP for the sëlection of representative Web services. With 1 increase in the number of services puЬliës on the Web, choosing a service from several candidates that offer the same functionatitë with different QoS has become a crucial problem. The Skyline method has emerged in recent years as a new paradigm for choosing the best Web services [Borzsonyi 2001] [Benouaret et al 2012] [Yu et al, 2009], it is seen as a promising direction for reducing the user's decision space by preësëlecting the best Web services and discarding other dominated Web services. However, the dominance relation used by Skyline has some drawbacks: (i) the size of the Skyline result cannot be controlled, in fact, the Skyline result can be large and greedy which requires a lot of effort to process, as it can be very small and inconsistent for the user, (ii) Skyline generally returns conflicting and incomparable results which makes the sëlection process very difficult for the user, (iii) Skyline places the same importance on the sëlection cirières (QoS), however, QoS differs from one context to another and from one user to another, for example, in the e-payment context, the sëcuritë criterion is more important than the other criteria, but in the information retrieval context, response time is the most important criterion.

To control the size of the Skyline result, the K-representative Skyline concept has ëlë proposedë by [Lin et al., 2007] [Tao et al., 2009], this variant of Skyline allows to return a subset of the Skyline result that represents the totality of the Skyline result. № Nevertheless, this variant returns a set of QoS conflicting and incomparable Web services, where, the user finds difficulties in choosing the best services that meet their needs [Ouadah et al., 2018b] [Ouadah et al., 2018c],.

The approach of using multi-criteria decision support methods (MCDMs) for ranking alternatives is not new, AHP (Analytical Hierarchy Process) and Fuzzy AHP represent the most widely used methods as a decision support tool in several domains for the sëlection of services, customers, matëriels, ëquipements, consumers, ...etc [Chang 1996] [Godse et al., 2008] [Kwong et al., 2002]. The main advantage of AHP and Fuzzy AHP lies in their ability: (1) to be combined with other multi-criteria decision support methods, (2) to evaluate quantitative and qualitative measures, and (3) to be used in conjunction with other decision support methods.

(3) to verify the consistency of users' judgements. Several approaches have been proposed in the literature, combining the AHP method with other MCDMs such as PROMETHEE [Macharis et al., 2004] [Wang et al., 2007] [Karim et al., 2011], Electre [Kaya et al, 2011], Topsis [Buyukozkan et a., 2012] [Onut et al., 2008], Fuzzy Topsis [Barrios et a., 2016], Skyline and PROMETHEE [Ouadah et al, 2015 a, b], Skyline, Entropy and PROMETHEE [Ouadah et al., 2018a]. However, AHP and Fuzzy AHP require the completion of several comparison matrices between criteria and between alternatives according to their importance expressed as a Saaty scale (1-9), which requires a lot of effort from the user and makes them very difficult to use in practice, especially in the field of Web service selection, where the number of published services increases daily. Few studies have focused on the automatic generation of comparison matrices between criteria and variants, using performance matrix data. The only work we found is by Nefeslioglu et al [Nefeslioglu et al., 2013], where, the authors propose a modified version of the AHP method, where, the user is asked to give a score for each range of values of each criterion, which represents a kind of manual data discretization. This approach requires a great deal of effort from the user and is very difficult to use, especially when the number of alternatives is very large, as in the field of Web service selection.

With the AHP and Fuzzy AHP methods, the user has to redo all the work of reconstructing these comparison matrices if the consistency test fails (the consistency ratio exceeds the value 0.1), which is a tedious task, particularly when the number of criteria and alternatives is very large.

To overcome these drawbacks, we propose a hybrid approach:

- The Skyline result is segmented into k clusters in order to identify the set of K-representative Skyline Web services, which represents the totality of the Skyline result and gives the user a summary view of the entire Skyline result.
- An improved version of the Fuzzy AHP method is proposed in order to: (1) weight QoS criteria based on the explicitness of user preferences using a set of linguistic terms and minimising user effort, (2) group QoS criteria according to their degree of importance in order to reduce the number of binary comparisons between QoS criteria, (3) automatically generate priority vectors for each criterion, from QoS data, using a discretisation algorithm, (4) rank Skyline k-representative Web services in order to provide the user with a short list of relevant Web services that best meet their needs.

5.4.1 Motivating example

Consider the following example, which illustrates the relevance of using the Skyline method. Considerërons un ensemble de services Web qui offrent la même fonctionalite de paiement électronique avec des QoS differentes, ces services fournissent aux utilisateurs un moyen très rapide de réservation et paiement on line. In this example, two QoS criteria are considered: *response time* and *security*. Assume that the QoS data is normalized and both criteria are minimized (minimum values are preferred). The user searches for relevant Web services with respect to the two QoS criteria of *response time* and *security*, and the Skyline result, which represents the most relevant Web services, is illustrated in Figure 23.

Table 20. QoS data.

Service	QoS
S_1	(0.6, 0.5)
S_2	(0.1, 0.8)
S_3	(0.7, 0.2)
S_4	(0.3, 0.8)
S_5	(0.2, 0.6)
S_6	(0.7, 0.9)
S_7	(0.3, 1.0)
S_8	(0.4, 0.4)
S_9	(0.8, 0.1)
S_{10}	(0.3, 0.3)
S_{11}	(0.25, 0.4)

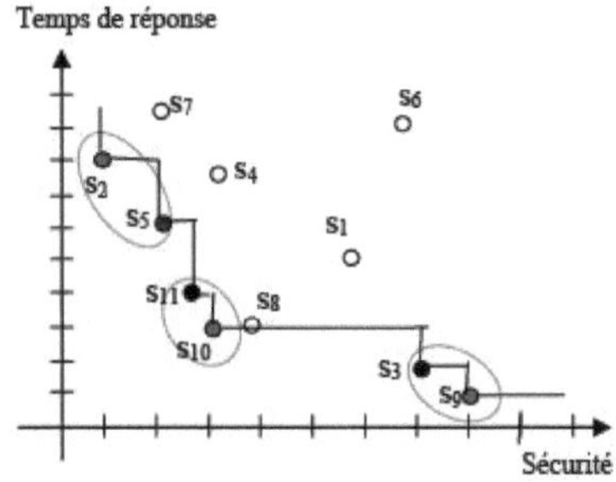

Figure 23. K-representative Skyline Web Services.

One of the main features of the Skyline operator is that it gives the same importance to all the criteria. However, the weights of the criteria are very relevant in several areas and vary from one area to another and from one context to another. For example, in e-commerce, the *security* criterion is given priority over the other criteria. In the example above, the Skyline s_2 web service represents the most secure service, while the s_{10} web service has a good compromise between the two criteria. Whereas in the information retrieval domain, the user is looking for the best service in terms of *response time*, as is the case for the s_9 Web service. Consequently, QoS criteria must be classified according to the user's preferences. Furthermore, given the difficulty of controlling the number of Web services returned by Skyline, the user needs to have a summary that represents all the Skyline results. The Skyline K-representative variant meets this need by returning the most relevant Skyline Web services. In this example, assuming K=3, this approach should return s_2, s_{10} and s_9.

s_2: the most sëcurisë Skyline web service.
s_{10}: the Skyline Web service with the best compromise between QoS criteria.
s_9: the best Skyline Web service in terms of response time.
However, the Web services returned by the K-representative Skyline mëthod (the dots in red, see Figure 23) are incomparable and conflicting, so the user must express his preferences on the QoS criteria in order to rank the Web services according to his preferences.

5.4.2 Improved Fuzzy AHP (IFAHP) approach :

The IFAHP approach we are proposing meets the following objectives:

(1) Reduction of the search space, offering the user only those Web services which are not dominated by any other service and which represent a summary of the global Skyline result.

(2) Proposal of an improved version of the Fuzzy AHP method, which offers the following contributions:

- The expression of preferences relating to the levels of importance of QoS criteria using linguistic terms;
- The grouping of QoS criteria that have the same level of importance, in order to reduce the number of comparisons between QoS criteria in the weighting phase;
- Automatic generation of comparison matrices between Skyline Web services with respect

to each QoS criterion using the discretisation of the performance matrix (QoS data);

- Storage of Skyline K-representatives web services.

The stages of the IFAHP approach (see Figure 24) are described as follows:

In the first step, the Skyline operator is used to discard irrelevant Web services and focus on the best services that are not dominated by any other service. Next, the Skyline result is segmented into a set of k clusters, based on the K-means method, the best Skyline Web service from each cluster will be proposed to the user.

In the second step, we propose an improved version of the Fuzzy AHP method in order to calculate the weights of the QoS criteria and rank the k-representative Skyline Web services.

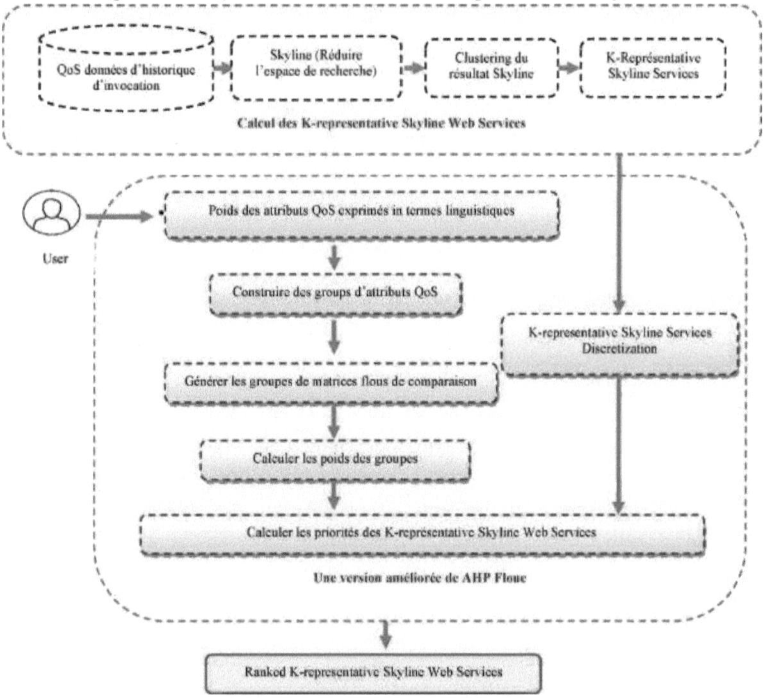

Figure 24. The IFAHP approach.

5.4.2.1 Calculation of Skyline k-representative Web services

The Skyline operator is a popular and relevant tool for modelling and processing preferences in databases [Borzsonyi et al., 2001]. Given $p_i, p_2, \ldots p_n$ a set of objects, the Skyline operator returns the set of objects p_i that are not dominated by any other objects p_j. The Skyline operator is based on the Pareto dominance relation, which can be formalised as follows:

Given s_i and $S_j \in S$, s_i is said to dominate s_j, denoted by $s_i < s_j$, if and only if Si is better than or equal to s_j on all QoS criteria and better strictly on a single QoS criterion. The Skyline result of a set of Web Services *S*, with similar functionality, represent the subset s_i that are not dominated by any other Web Service s_j in *S*.

$$\forall u \in [1,m],\ G_u(S_i) \leq G_u(S_j) \land \exists\, v \in [1,m],\ G_v(S_i) < G_v(S_j)$$

Skyline K-reprOsentative is a variant of Skyline that returns a summary of the overall Skyline result to the user [Lin et al., 2007] [Tao et al., 2009]. It considerably reduces the size of the Skyline result, returning only the most relevant Web services.

5.4.2.1.1 Calculating the Skyline result

The Skyline operator is used to reduce the search space and focus on Web services that are not dominated by any other service. The BNL (Block Nested Loops) algorithm [Borzsonyi et al., 2001] is used to calculate the Skyline result due to its simplicity and ease of use.

5.4.2.1.2 Segmentation of Skyline results

The K-means method is used to segment the Skyline output into k segments, each segment will contain Skyline web services that are similar to each other and dissimilar in comparison to the Skyline web services in the other segments.

K-means is the most widely used segmentation method in the literature [Jain 2010], and is simple, easy to use and efficient. The main stages of the K-means method are :

1- Choose the number of segments K to be composed and the distance calculation function;

Repeat steps 2 and 3 until the segments are stable;

2- GOnOrer a new segment by assigning each Skyline web service to the segment closest to the segment centre ;

3- Calculate the new segment centres;

5.4.2.1.3 SOlection of K-reprOsentative Skyline Web services

In this approach, we propose to choose a Skyline Web service from each segment, the one closest to the centre of the segment. This will enable us to select the Web service with the best compromise between the QoS criteria within the segment.

We use the Euclidean mOthod to calculate the distances between the Skyline web services and the centres of the segments.

5.4.2.2 Description of the new version of Fuzzy AHP

In this section we will dëcribe the new version of Fuzzy AHP based on its different ëtapes [Ouadah et al., 2018d]. It consists in: making explicit the importance of QoS criteria, grouping them according to their importance, calculating the weights of these criteria, discretising the QoS data, generating the comparison matrices, and finally, arranging the Skyline Web Services.

5.4.2.2.1 Explaining the importance of QoS criteria

The importance of the QoS criteria is formulated by the user based on the following linguistic terms. The user must associate a specific level of importance with each criterion:

Table 21. Linguistic terms.

Linguistic terms	Definition
VI	Tres important (Very important)
I	Important
N	Normal
NI	Not Important
NIA	Not Important at All

5.4.2.2.2 Grouping of QoS criteria

Grouping QoS criteria involves assigning all criteria of the same importance to the same group. We assume that criteria belonging to the same group will have the same weight.

The QoS criteria are grouped into five groups according to their importance, noted as follows: $G_i = (G_1, G_2, ..., G_5)$. or :

G1 contains the most important QoS criteria (*VI*) ;

G2 contains the Important QoS criteria (*I*) ;
G3 contains QoS criteria that have the same importance Normal (N) ;
G4 contains the non-important (*NI*) QoS criteria;
G5 contains the non-important QoS criteria (*NIA*).
In the example described in section (5.4.1), if the level of importance given by the user on the two criteria *security* and *response time* are respectively VI (very important) and NI (not important), then the two criteria will belong to two different groups G1 and G4, or, G1 = {security} and G4 = {response time}.
5.4.2.2.3 Generation of the comparison matrix between groups
The comparison matrix between the groups can be constructed using the dependency matrix (DEP) between the linguistic terms. This matrix expresses the relationship between two linguistic terms using triangular fuzzy numbers (TFN):

$$DEP = \begin{array}{c} \\ VI \\ I \\ N \\ NI \\ NIA \end{array} \begin{array}{c} \begin{array}{ccccc} VI & I & N & NI & NIA \end{array} \\ \begin{bmatrix} 1 & \tilde{3} & \tilde{5} & \tilde{7} & \tilde{9} \\ \tilde{3}^{-1} & 1 & \tilde{3} & \tilde{5} & \tilde{7} \\ \tilde{5}^{-1} & \tilde{3}^{-1} & 1 & \tilde{3} & \tilde{5} \\ \tilde{7}^{-1} & \tilde{5}^{-1} & \tilde{3}^{-1} & 1 & \tilde{3} \\ \tilde{9}^{-1} & \tilde{7}^{-1} & \tilde{5}^{-1} & \tilde{3}^{-1} & 1 \end{bmatrix} \end{array}$$

The intensity of importance between linguistic terms is expressed in triangular fuzzy numbers (TFN) according to the following comparison scale:
Table 22: Comparison scale between linguistic terms.

Fuzzy numbers	Definition	Function
T	Equal importance	(1,1,2)
3	Moderate importance	(2,3,4)
5	Great importance	(4,5,6)
7	Very important	(6,7,8)
9	Extreme importance	(8,9,10)

The dependency matrix can be described as follows: a very important QoS criterion (VI) has the same importance as another very important criterion (VI), a very important QoS criterion (VI) has moderate importance over another important QoS criterion (I), a very important QoS criterion (VI) has extreme importance over another QoS criterion that is not important at all (NIA), ...etc.
In the example in section (5.4.1), the comparison between the two groups G1 (which contains the most important QoS criteria) and G4 (which contains the unimportant QoS criteria) is given as follows:

$$CM(G_1,G_4) = \begin{array}{c} \\ G_1 \\ G_4 \end{array} \begin{array}{c} \begin{array}{cc} G_1 & G_4 \end{array} \\ \begin{bmatrix} \tilde{1} & \tilde{7} \\ \tilde{7}^{-1} & \tilde{1} \end{bmatrix} \end{array}$$

5.4.2.2.4 Calculation of weights for groups of QoS criteria
Now that the comparison matrix is gënërëe, the weights of the groups of criteria can be calculated following the steps of the Fuzzy AHP method described in section 4.2.2.
5.4.2.2.5 Discretisation of the performance matrix

With Fuzzy AHP, in order to calculate the priority of alternatives with respect to each QoS criterion, the user is required to fill in a set of comparison matrices, which requires a great deal of effort, particularly when the number of alternatives is very large. To overcome this drawback, we propose to automatically generate the comparison matrices between Skyline Web services with respect to each criterion, by means of an algorithm for discretising the performance matrix containing the QoS data of the k-representative Skyline Web services.
According to [Garcia et al., 2013], discretisation makes it possible to transform quantitative data into qualitative data, numerical criteria into discrete or nominal criteria with a finite number of intervals. In practice, discretisation can be seen as a method of data reduction, mapping data from a broad spectrum of numerical values to a highly reduced subset of discrete values.
In our approach, we will follow the following process for the discretization of QoS data:
Step 1: data normalisation: in this step, the QoS data is normalised so that the largest value is the one that will be preferred.
For negative QoS criteria, the highest value is preferred (e.g. security):

$$NG_J(S_i) = \frac{max - G_J(S_i)}{max - min} \quad (5.1)$$

For positive QoS criteria, the smallest value is preferred (e.g. response time):

$$(5.2) \quad NG_J(S_i) = \frac{G_J(S_i) - min}{max - min}$$

Step 2: Discretisation: In this step, we transform the continuous values into discretes, using the equal-width method [Dougherty et al., 1995], which partitions the continuous QoS criteria into K intervals using the following algorithm:

Algorithm 5.3 Discretization of QoS data
***Input**: QoS data, number of K slots.*
Foreach** QoS criteria **do
Calculate the width of each interval using the following function:
*[min + (k-1)*w, min+k*w]*
By these means :
The first interval is: [min, min+w].
*oŭ : min + k*w = max.*
QoS data labelling: using linguistic terms.
***End**.*
***Return** QoS data*

In this approach, we propose a value of k = 5, where each interval expresses a level of importance, as follows:

Table 23. Labelling of QoS data.

Intervals	Label	Description
[min, min+w[	VI	Very important
[min+w, min+2*w[	I	Important
[min+2*w, min+3*w[	N	Normal
[min+3*w, min+4*w[	NI	Not Important
[min+4*w, min+5*w]	NIA	Not Important for everything

The QoS data labelling operation allows the level of importance of each Skyline Web Service to be described in relation to each QoS criterion. Importance in this case means the relevance of the Skyline Web Service with respect to that QoS criterion.

In our example, we assume that k=5, so w= (1-0)/5 =0.2. The QoS data for Skyline Web Services can be discretised as follows:

Table 24. Example of QoS data discretisation.

Skyline Web Service	Response time	Response time label	Security	Security label
S2	0.1	VI	0.8	NIA
S10	0.3	I	0.3	I
S9	0.8	NIA	0.1	VI

As can be seen from Table 24, the Skyline S2 web service is very important in terms of the *response time* criterion, but it is not important in terms of the security criterion. The Skyline Web service S10 is important in terms of both QoS criteria. The Skyline S9 web service is very important for *security* but not for *response time.*

5.4.2.2.6 Calculating priorities

In this step, we exploit the discretized data to generate the binary comparison matrices between each two Skyline Web Services, with respect to each QoS criterion. To do this, we use the dependency matrix between the linguistic terms and follow the same procedure described in section 6.4.2.2.3.

In the previous example, and in order to generate the priority vector between the two Skyline Web services *S2* and *S10,* with regard to the *response time* criterion, the *S2* service is labelled as very important (VI), *S10* is labelled as important (I). Therefore, the comparison between the two Web services in terms of response time corresponds to the comparison between the two linguistic terms VI and I, given as follows:

$$CM(S_2,S_{10}) = \begin{array}{c} \\ S_2 \\ S_{10} \end{array}\begin{array}{c} \begin{array}{cc} S_2 & S_{10} \end{array} \\ \begin{bmatrix} \tilde{1} & \tilde{3} \\ \tilde{3}^{-1} & \tilde{1} \end{bmatrix} \end{array}$$

Once the binary comparison matrices have been generated automatically, the priority vectors can be calculated using the classic Fuzzy AHP procedure proposed by [Chang 1996].

5.4.2.2.7 Priority Summary and Ranking of Skyline Web Service k-representative After calculating the weights of the QoS criteria and the Skyline Web Service priority vectors, the latter can be ranked on the basis of the score calculated as follows:

$$\text{IFAHP Score}_i = \sum_j QoS\ Eigenvector_j \times W_i \qquad (5.3)$$

5.5 Conclusion

In this chapter we have presented the approaches proposed to overcome the problems identified at the beginning of this thesis. Firstly, we presented the SkyAP-S3 approach, which combines three multi-criteria decision support methods: Skyline for the reduction of the search space, AHP for the weighting of QoS criteria and PROMETHEE for the ranking of Skyline Web services, making it possible to offer the user a shortlist of Web services that best meet their preferences. Next, we presented the SEFAP (Skyline, Entropy, Fuzzy AHP and PROMETHEE) approach, an improved version of SkyAP-S3, which addresses the problem of subjectivity and imprecision in the user's opinion when weighting QoS criteria, the Entropy method is used to extract the weights of QoS criteria from QoS data, while Fuzzy AHP, addresses the imprecision and subjectivity in user opinions through l'integration de la thcorie de l'ensemble fuoue. The latest approach appelëe IFAHP, proposes a new version of the Fuzzy AHP mëthod, to remëdier the inconvënients prësentës by classical Fuzzy AHP, This new version automatically manages the different comparison matrices between criteria and between alternatives in order to minimise the user's efforts when weighting QoS criteria and ranking the k-representative Skyline Web services.

6 Implementation and Experimentation

6.1 Presentation of the Prototype

In this section we present the prototype called SEFAP (Skyline Web Services Ranking). We begin by describing the modules that make up the prototype, namely: loading QoS data, calculating the Skyline result, calculating subjective and objective weights, and partial and complete ranking of Skyline Web services.

Figure 25 gives an overview of the prototype.

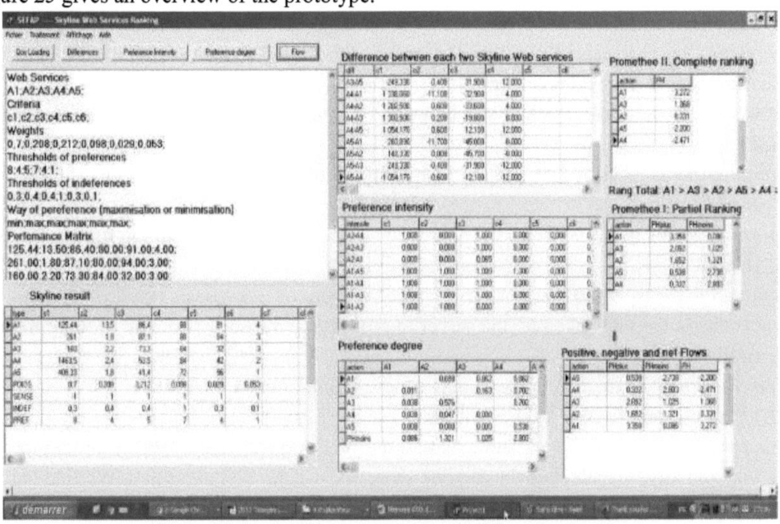

Figure 25. Prototype produced as part of the experiments.

1- Loading data :

This function has been developed to load the databases: QWS Dataset and NBA Dataset, used during the experimentation phases.

2- Skyline calculation module :

Calculates the Skyline query for a set of data.

3- Organising Web services

This function calculates and displays :

- the difference between the two Skyline web services on all criteria.
- I intensite de prëfërences entre deux services Web Skyline sur tous les criteres ;
- The degree of preference between two Skyline ;
- Positive, negative and net flows;
- Ranking of Skyline web services by net flow.

An additional function is added to calculate the execution time for each stage.

Certain simulations and the generation of graphical reports were carried out in Excel.

6.2 Experimental study of the SkyAP-S3 and SEFAP approaches :

In this section, we present an experimental evaluation of the SkyAP-S3 and SEFAP approaches. Our experimental study was carried out on a PC with a 2.01 Ghz, 2.09 Ghz core duo CPU and 2 GB of RAM. We used two public databases, QWS Dataset and NBA Dataset.

6.2.1 QWS Dataset database

The objective of this database is to provide Web services researchers with a set of data for experimenting their work. It is a public database proposed by [Al-masri et al., 2007], it provides a set of 365 real Web services, which currently exist on the Web, it includes measurements of nine QoS criteria:

Response time: this is the time taken between the client sending the request and the Web service receiving the response. The unit of measurement is ms (milliseconds).

Availability: this is measured by the ratio between the number of successful invocations and the total number of invocations.

Throughput: this represents the number of invocations during a given period of time. The unit of measurement is (invocations/second).

Success: this is measured by the ratio between the number of responses and the number of requests.

Reliability: this is measured by the ratio between the number of error messages and the total number of messages.

Conformance: this is measured by the degree to which the WSDL description file conforms to W3C spëcifications.

Best practice: the extent to which a service takes account of WS-I Basic Proiile

Latency: this is the time taken by the server to process the message. The unit of measurement is ms (milliseconds).

Documentation: documentation measure (i.e. description of tags) for WSDL

6.2.1.1 Calculating Skyline Web Services

In this experimental study, we assume that all the Web services in the QWS Dataset offer the same functionality. To calculate the Skyline score, we use the BNI algorithm. We find that the Skyline result varies according to the number of QoS criteria. For eight criteria, the Skyline result returns 117 Web services out of 2507 offered, for 3 and 4 criteria the Skyline result returns only 12 Web services out of 2507.

While varying the number of QoS criteria to be taken into account in calculating the Skyline result from 3 to 9, the size of the Skyline result changes accordingly (see figure 26).

It can be seen that the search space has been reduced considerably for the user to enable them to focus only on relevant Web services that are not dominated by any other service. For example, for eight QoS criteria, the search space is reduced from 2507 Web services to 117 Web services only, representing 1/21 of the initial space. Reducing the decision space will make it much easier for the user during the selection phase. Furthermore, it can be noted that the Skyline result increases considerably with the increase in the number of QoS criteria.

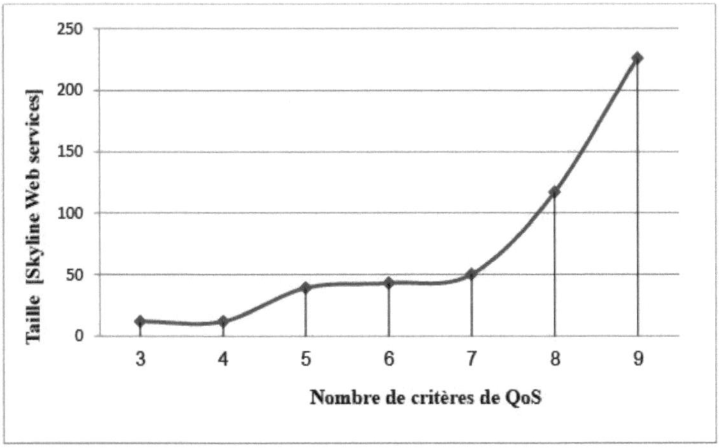

Figure 26. Skyline result size according to the number of QoS criteria.

6.2.1.2 Ranking of Skyline Web Services

Table 25 and Figure 27 illustrate the top-10 Skyline web services taking into account six QoS criteria: (Q1*: Response time*, Q2: *Availability*, Q3: *Throughput*, Q4: *Successibility*, Q5: *Reliability*, Q6*: Conformance*, Q7: *Good practice*, Q8: *Latency*), the result shows that both SkyAP-S3 and SEFAP can capture user preferences and return the most relevant Skyline Web Services with the best compromise between QoS criteria.

Ranking of Skyline services

Ranking of services Skyline

Service	PHplus	PHmoins	PH
A1161	80,773	14,793	60,979
A832	79,606	15,562	64,044
A1610	71,319	26,386	44,933
A2200	70,403	27,326	43,077
A1556	69,925	27,426	42,499
A760	67,037	29,288	37,750
A170	64,539	27,815	36,725
A1482	66.589	30.220	36.369
A462	65.473	29.480	35.994
A1390	60,936	35,203	33,733
A787	65,884	32,394	33,490

Figure 27. Result of arranging Skyline Web services.

Table 25. Top-10 Skyline web services.

Rank	Service	Q1	Q2	Q3	Q4	Q5	Q6	Q7	Q8
1st	S1161	41	97	43,1	99	73	100	84	1
2nd	S832	57	98	34,6	100	73	100	84	1
3rd	S1610	80	99	36,3	100	80	100	87	13
4th	S2200	78	100	35,3	100	67	78	72	1
5th	S1556	65	99	31,6	100	80	89	65	21
6th	S760	68,83	100	21,4	100	73	100	80	7,33
7th	S170	63,8	99	18,1	100	73	78	84	1,8
8th	S1482	71,16	99	21,9	100	78	89	89	16,44
9th	S462	99	99	31,1	100	73	100	84	2

10th	S1390	57	91	27,3	97	83	89	93	14

6.2.1.3 Performance evaluation

From the performance evaluation result, we can see that the execution time for ordering Skyline Web services increases considërabIement with the increase in the size of the Skyline result, this is justifiedë by the time taken to calculate the intensity of prëfërences and the degree of preference between each two Skyline Web services. We note that this exëcution time has been reduced considerably by reducing the search space, this will avoid comparing Skyline Web services with non-Skyline Web services. On the other hand, if the PROMETHEE method used for Skyline Web services ordering, is applied directly on the total QoS data (2507) as it has been proposed by existing approaches [Karim et al 2011] [Vesyropoulos et al. 2015][Seo et al. 2005], the execution time will increase in a very significant way.

Figure 28 shows that reducing the search space using the Skyline method overcomes the computational time limitations of multicriteria decision support methods such as PROMETHEE [Marinoni 2006]. For example, with eight QoS criteria, the search space was reduced from 2507 Web services to 117 Skyline Web services only, which improved the computational performance of the proposed approaches: SkyAP-S3 and SEFAP.

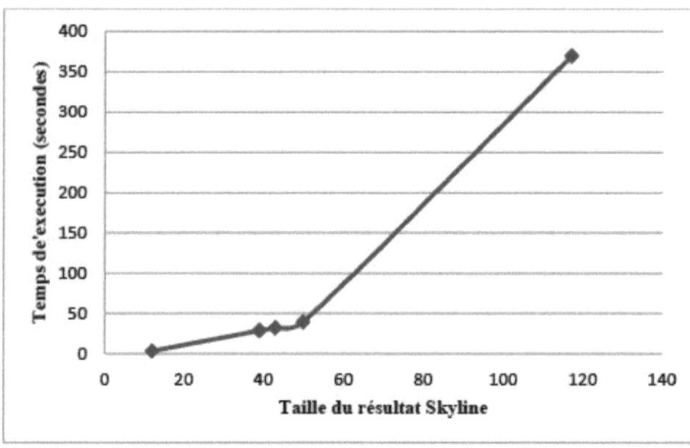

Figure 28. Evaluation of the performance of the Skyline Web services.

6.2.1.4 Sensitivity Analysis of QoS Criteria Weights

The sensitivity analysis given in table 26, provides for each QoS criterion the lower and upper bounds between which the weights of the criteria can be varied without altering the total top10- ranking of Skyline web services.

Table 26. Sensitivity analysis of QoS weights.

Criteria	Q1	Q2	Q3	Q4	Q5	Q6	Q7	Q8
Weight	0,320	0,250	0,150	0,020	0,070	0,050	0,040	0,100
Min	0,299	0,241	0,000	0,010	0,000	0,000	0,041	0,098
Max	0,344	0,281	0,166	0,059	0,101	0,068	0,020	0,101

From table 26, we can see that the weights of criteria Q8: Latency and Q2: Availability have a high impact on the ranking of Skyline Web services. Criteria Q5: Reliability and Q6:

Conformance have a medium impact, while the other criteria have an acceptable impact.

6.2.2 NBA DataSet database

The NBA Dataset database contains 21,961 records, a set of statistics relating to 17 characteristics (criteria) of NBA players during the seasons from 1946 to 2009.

In order to make comparisons with existing approaches, we selected the following ten criteria: points scored (*PTS:* Points Scored), total rebounds (*REB:* Rebounds), assists (*AST:* Assists), 2-point field goals (*FGM: Field Goal Made*), Total Steals (*STL: Steals*), Blocks (*Blk: Blocks*), *Field Goals At*tempted *(FGA: Field Goals Attempted), Field Goals Made (FGM: Field Goals Made*), Free Throws Attempted (*FTA*: Free Throws Attempted), Free Throws Made (*FTM*: Free Throws Made). The Skyline method returned 252 players out of 21,961.

6.2.2.1 Weighting of criteria

The weights of the criteria were calculated by comparing each two criteria using the Saaty scale (1-9). The binary comparison matrix between the criteria is given as follows:

Table 27. Weighting of NBA player criteria.

	P T	R E	A S	F C	F T	F T	S T	B L	T C	F C	V e
PTS	1	2	3	3	5	2	3	4	4	4	**0,23**
REB	1/2	1	3	3	2	3	3	2	2	2	**0,18**
ASTS	1/3	1/3	1	2	3	3	4	2	1	2	**0,14**
FGM	1/3	1/3	1/3	1	1/5	1/4	1/3	1/5	1	2	**0,03**
FTA	1/5	1/2	1/3	2	1	2	3	1/2	2	1	**0,08**
FTM	1/2	1/2	1/4	4	1/2	1	2	1/3	2	1	**0,08**
STL	1/3	1/3	1/4	3	1/3	1/2	1	1/3	2	3	**0,05**
BLK	1/4	1/2	1/2	5	2	3	3	1	2	3	**0,13**
TOV	1/4	1/2	1/5	1/5	1/2	1/3	1/2	1/2	1	1/3	**0,04**
FGA	1/4	1/5	1/4	1/3	1	1	1	1/2	3	1	**0,04**

6.2.2.2 NBA player rankings

Once the criteria had been weighted, the NBA players were ranked using the ranking algorithm proposed in the SEFAP approaches.

The result of Skyline player ranking depends on the preferences expressed by the user (preference and indifference thresholds) and the weights assigned to the ten criteria. Comparing the ranking result of our approach with existing approaches [Dai et al. 2013][Vlachou et al. 2010].

Table 28. Comparison between SEFAP and other approaches.

Order	SEFAP	Skyline frequency	Skyrank
1st	G. Mcginnis 1974	Mr Jordan1986	G. Mcginnis 1974
2nd	Mr Jordan 1988	G. Mcginnis 1974	H. Olajuwon 1988
3rd	J. Erving 1975	Mr Jordan1987	C. Barkley1985
4th	J. Erving 1973	W. Chamb.1961	H. Olajuwon 1989
5th	J. Erving 1974	C. Barkley 1987	C. Barkley 1987
6th	Mr Jordan 1987	C. Barkley 1985	Mr Jordan1987
7th	Mr Malone 1981	M. Richardson 1979	A. Iverson 2004
8th	W. Chamb.1963	H. Olajuwon1988	Mr Jordan 1986
9th	Mr Jordan 1986	H. Olajuwon1989	J. Stackhouse 2000
10th	Mr Jordan 1989	Mr Jordan 1988	D. Robinson 1993

In the Skyline player ranking result shown in Table 28, we see that most of the players returned by the *Skyline frequency* and *SKYRANK* approaches were returned by our SEFAP approach.

6.2.2.3 Performance evaluation

To assess the performance of the SEFAP approach compared with existing approaches (*Skyline frequency* and *Skyrank*) on the basis of NBA Dataset data, we use the DCG (Discounted Cumulative Gain) indicator [Jarvelin el al. 2002], which is often used as a proxy for the SEFAP approach.

a performance indicator for storage results.

$$DCG_k = \sum_{i=1}^{k} \frac{rel_i}{log_2(i+1)} \tag{6.1}$$

Knowing that rel_i is given by the following equation :

$$rel_i = \sum_{j=1}^{n} W_i * Q_i \tag{6.2}$$

The value of the DCG indicator is accumulated from the top of the rankings to the bottom with the gain of each expected result in the lower ranks, a high value of DCG means a high quality of rankings of NBA Skyline players.

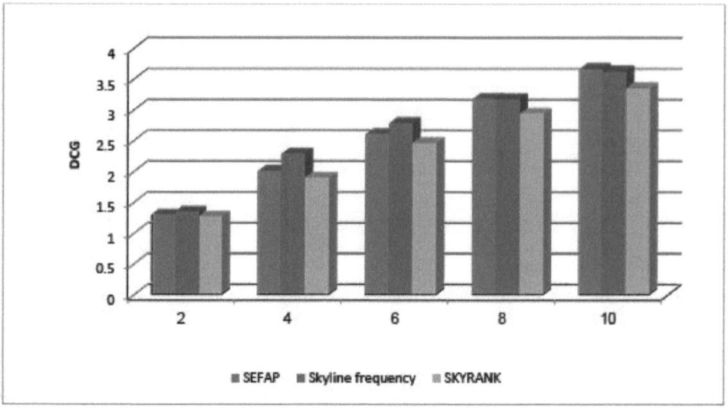

Figure 29. DCG of the Top-10 Skyline players in the NBA.

Figure 29, shows that the SEFAP approach obtains superior DCG values compared to *Skyline frequency* and *Skyrank* for the top-10. The *Skyline frequency* approach obtains better values for the ranking of top-04 and top-06. Also, the DCG indicator obtained for SEFAP becomes more ёкуё when the number of Skyline players becomes larger.

6.3 Experimental Study of the IFAHP Approach

In this section, we present an experimental study of the IFAHP approach using the public database QWS Dataset.

6.3.1 Calculating Skyline Web Services

We consider that the Web services in the QWS Dataset database offer the same functionality. We use eight QoS criteria: Q1*: response time*, Q2: *availability*, Q3: *throughput*, Q4: *success*, Q5: *reliability*, Q6: *compliance*, Q7: *good practice*, Q8*: latency*.

The Skyline method returns 117 Skyline Web services out of 2507 proposed by the QWS Dataset database. We note that the search space is considerably reduced, with only those Web services that are not dominated by any other Web service being proposed to the user. We note that despite this reduction in the number of Web services, it is still difficult for the user to choose a service from among the 117 offered.

One proposal is to calculate the Skyline Web services per domain. For the SOAP domain, the Skyline result returns 55 Web services out of 464 offered. For the *Search* domain, Skyline returns 23 Skyline Web services out of 100 offered.

Finally, for e-commerce, the Skyline method returns 24 of the 30 services offered.

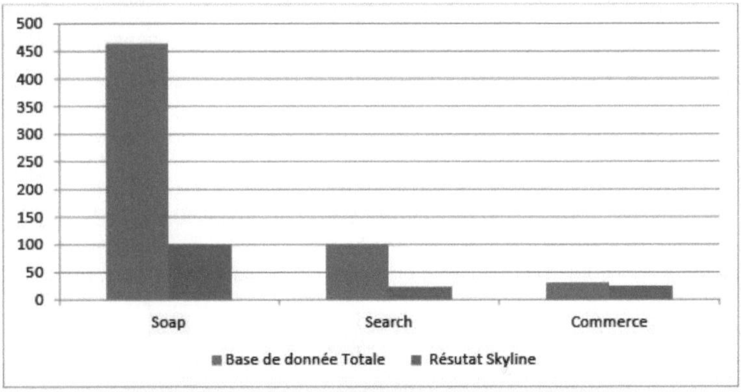

Figure 30. Calculation of Skyline Web services by domain.

Another proposal is to segment the Skyline result into a set of segments, and offer the user a short list of Web services that represents a summary of all the proposed Skyline Web services.

6.3.2 Selection of Skyline k-representatives Web Services

In this ëtape, we segment the Skyline result into a set of K segments (in our case, we use k=10). Each segment contains Skyline Web Services that are similar to each other. We calculate the distance between each Skyline Web Service and the centroid of the segment in order to offer the user only one Web service per segment, the one closest to the centroid of the segment.

The Skyline k-representative Web services are shown in the following table:

Table 29. Skyline k-representatives Web services.

Segment No.	Number of services	Representatives Skyline
1	8	S447
2	10	S1541
3	7	S20
4	16	S2125
5	14	S1736
6	12	S1295
7	18	S823
8	6	S2104
6	23	S1371
10	3	S236

6.3.3 Weighting of QoS Criteria

To choose a Web service from among several available Web services, the user was asked to express his or her priorities with regard to QoS criteria, using linguistic terms as illustrated in

Figure 31.

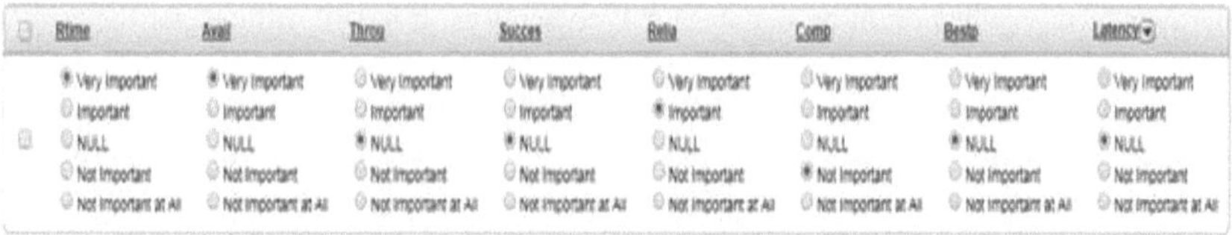

Figure 31. Expression of priorities based on QoS criteria.

We consider that the importance of the QoS criteria expressed by the user is given in table 30. The QoS criteria are grouped according to their importance. Four groups are formed: *G1 = {Q1, Q2}*, *G2 = {Q3, Q4, Q7, Q8}*, *G3 = {Q5}*, *G4 = {Q6}*.

$$CM = \begin{array}{c} \\ G_1 \\ G_2 \\ G3 \\ G_4 \end{array} \begin{array}{c} \begin{array}{cccc} G_1 & G_2 & G_3 & G_4 \end{array} \\ \begin{bmatrix} 1 & \tilde{5} & \tilde{3} & \tilde{7} \\ \tilde{5}^{-1} & 1 & \tilde{3}^{-1} & \tilde{3} \\ \tilde{3}^{-1} & \tilde{3} & 1 & \tilde{5} \\ \tilde{7}^{-1} & \tilde{3}^{-1} & \tilde{5}^{-1} & 1 \end{bmatrix} \end{array}$$

The weights of the criteria are calculated; QoS criteria belonging to the same group will have the same weight.

We find that the process of weighting QoS criteria requires less effort from the user. In our case, for eight QoS criteria, the user is asked to express their priorities on the level of importance of each criterion by pressing linguistic terms, and as a consëquence, the weights will be calculated directly in a simple and intuitive way. With conventional AHP and Fuzzy AHP methods, the user is required to fill in a comparison matrix composed of 64 entries, which is very difficult in practice.

Table 30. Weighting of QoS criteria.

QoS criteria	Q1	Q2	Q3	Q4	Q5	Q6	Q7	Q8
Importance	VI	VI	N	N	I	NI	N	N
Groups of criteria	G1	G1	G2	G2	G3	G4	G2	G2
Weight	0,28	0,28	0,12	0,12	0,2	0,04	0,12	0,12

6.3.4 Discretisation of QoS Data

To calculate priority vectors for Skyline Web services, we use a discretisation algorithm to transform continuous QoS data into discrete data. After the two steps of normalisation and labelling, the discretised QoS data is given as follows:

Table 31. Discretised QoS data.

	Q1	Q2	Q3	Q4	Q5	Q6	Q7	Q8
A447	VI	NI	VI	N	N	N	VI	I
A1541	I	I	NI	VI	NIA	VI	N	VI
A20	VI	N	NIA	VI	NI	NIA	N	VI
A2125	VI	I	NIA	VI	N	VI	I	NIA
A1736	NIA	I	NI	VI	I	N	VI	I
A1295	VI	NIA	NI	NIA	N	N	I	NI
A823	VI	I	N	VI	NI	NIA	N	VI
A2104	N	NIA	N	NIA	VI	NIA	VI	I
A1371	N	VI	I	VI	N	N	I	VI
A236	VI	N	I	VI	NIA	N	NIA	VI

6.3.5 Generation of comparison matrices for each QoS criterion

In this step, we exploit the QoS data discretised in the previous step, in order to generate the eight comparison matrices between Skyline Web services, with respect to each QoS criterion. To do this, we use the dependency matrix (DEP), which expresses the dependency between each two linguistic terms using triangular fuzzy numbers. For example, for QoS criterion Q1: *response time*, the comparison matrix between Skyline Web services is given as follows:

Tableau 32. The comparison matrix for the response time criterion.

Tableau 33.

	S_{447}	S_{1541}	S_{20}	S_{2125}	S_{1736}	S_{1295}	S_{823}	S_{2104}	S_{1371}	S_{236}
S_{447}	1	$\tilde{3}$	1	$\tilde{1}$	$\tilde{9}$	$\tilde{1}$	$\tilde{1}$	$\tilde{5}$	$\tilde{5}$	$\tilde{1}$
S_{1541}	$\tilde{3}^{-1}$	1	$\tilde{3}^{-1}$	$\tilde{3}^{-1}$	7	$\tilde{3}^{-1}$	$\tilde{3}^{-1}$	$\tilde{3}$	$\tilde{3}$	$\tilde{3}^{-1}$
S_{20}	$\tilde{1}^{-1}$	$\tilde{3}$	1	$\tilde{1}$	$\tilde{9}$	$\tilde{1}$	$\tilde{1}$	$\tilde{5}$	$\tilde{5}$	$\tilde{1}$
S_{2125}	$\tilde{1}^{-1}$	$\tilde{3}$	$\tilde{1}^{-1}$	1	$\tilde{9}$	$\tilde{1}$	$\tilde{1}$	$\tilde{5}$	$\tilde{5}$	$\tilde{1}$
S_{1736}	$\tilde{9}^{-1}$	7^{-1}	$\tilde{9}^{-1}$	$\tilde{9}^{-1}$	1	$\tilde{9}^{-1}$	$\tilde{9}^{-1}$	$\tilde{5}^{-1}$	$\tilde{5}^{-1}$	$\tilde{9}^{-1}$
S_{1295}	$\tilde{1}^{-1}$	$\tilde{3}$	$\tilde{1}^{-1}$	$\tilde{1}^{-1}$	$\tilde{9}$	1	$\tilde{1}$	$\tilde{5}$	$\tilde{5}$	$\tilde{1}$
S_{823}	$\tilde{1}^{-1}$	$\tilde{3}$	$\tilde{1}^{-1}$	$\tilde{1}^{-1}$	$\tilde{9}$	$\tilde{1}^{-1}$	1	$\tilde{5}$	$\tilde{5}$	$\tilde{1}$
S_{2104}	$\tilde{5}^{-1}$	$\tilde{3}^{-1}$	$\tilde{5}^{-1}$	$\tilde{5}^{-1}$	$\tilde{5}$	$\tilde{5}^{-1}$	$\tilde{5}^{-1}$	1	$\tilde{5}^{-1}$	$\tilde{5}^{-1}$
S_{1371}	$\tilde{5}^{-1}$	$\tilde{3}^{-1}$	$\tilde{5}^{-1}$	$\tilde{5}^{-1}$	$\tilde{5}$	$\tilde{5}^{-1}$	$\tilde{5}^{-1}$	$\tilde{5}$	1	$\tilde{5}^{-1}$
S_{236}	$\tilde{1}^{-1}$	$\tilde{3}$	$\tilde{1}^{-1}$	$\tilde{1}^{-1}$	$\tilde{9}$	$\tilde{1}^{-1}$	$\tilde{1}^{-1}$	$\tilde{5}$	$\tilde{5}$	1

Next, we assign the value 0.5 to a in equation (4.13), and the a-cut matrix is generated for each QoS criterion. The a-cut matrix for the *response time* criterion is generated (see Tables 33 and 34).

The consistency indicator (CI) is calculated as follows:

$$IC = (\lambda_{max} - N) / (N-1) = (10{,}91 - 10) / (10-1) = 0{,}10.$$

The consistency ratio (CR) is also :

RC = (IC / ACI) = (0.10 / 1.49) = 0.068.

We note that the consistency ratio (0.068) is less than 0.1.

Tableau 34. The a-cut comparison matrix for the response time criterion.

	S_{447}	S_{1541}	S_{20}	S_{2125}	S_{1736}	S_{1295}	S_{823}	S_{2104}	S_{1371}	S_{236}
S_{447}	1	[2,4]	[1,2]	[1,2]	[8,10]	[1,2]	[1,2]	[4,6]	[4,6]	[1,2]
S_{1541}	[1/4,1/2]	1	[1/4,1/2]	[1/4,1/2]	[6,8]	[1/4,1/2]	[1/4,1/2]	[2,4]	[2,4]	[1/4,1/2]
S_{20}	[1/2,1]	[2,4]	1	[1,2]	[8,10]	[1,2]	[1,2]	[4,6]	[4,6]	[1,2]
S_{2125}	[1/2,1]	[2,4]	[1/2,1]	1	[8,10]	[1,2]	[1,2]	[4,6]	[4,6]	[1,2]
S_{1736}	[1/10,1/8]	[1/8,1/6]	[1/10,1/8]	[1/10,1/8]	1	[1/10,1/8]	[1/10,1/8]	[1/6,1/4]	[1/6,1/4]	[1/10,1/8]
S_{1295}	[1/2,1]	[2,4]	[1/2,1]	[1/2,1]	[8,10]	1	[1,2]	[4,6]	[4,6]	[1,2]
S_{823}	[1/2,1]	[2,4]	[1/2,1]	[1/2,1]	[8,10]	[1/2,1]	1	[4,6]	[4,6]	[1,2]
S_{2104}	[1/6,1/4]	[1/4,1/2]	[1/6,1/4]	[1/2,1]	[4,6]	[1/6,1/4]	[1/6,1/4]	1	[1/6,1/4]	[1/6,1/4]
S_{1371}	[1/6,1/4]	[1/4,1/2]	[1/6,1/4]	[1/2,1]	[4,6]	[1/6,1/4]	[1/6,1/4]	[4,6]	1	[1/6,1/4]
S_{236}	[1/2,1]	[2,4]	[1/2,1]	[1/2,1]	[8,10]	[1/2,1]	[1/2,1]	[4,6]	[4,6]	1

Tableau 35. The priority vector for the response time QoS criterion.

	S447	S1541	S20	S2125	S1736	S1295	S823	S2104	S1371	S236	Eigenvector
S447	1	3	1,5	1,5	9	1,5	1,5	5	5		1,50,1692
S1541	0,375	1	0,375	0,375	7	0,375	0,375	3	3		0,3750,0619

S20	0,75	3	1	1,5	9	1,5	1,5	5	5		1,50,1570
S2125	0,75	3	0,75	1	9	1,5	1,5	5	5		1,50,1461
S1736	0,1125	0,14583	0,1125	0,1125	1	0,1125	0,1125	0,208	0,208	0,1125	0,0125
S1295	0,75	3	0,75	0,75	9		11,5	5	5		1,50,1363
S823	0,75	3	0,75	0,75	9	0,75		15	5		1,50,1273
S2104	0,208	0,375	0,208	0,208	5	0,208	0,208	1	0,208	0,208	0,0291
S1371	0,208	0,375	0,208	0,208	5	0,208	0,208	5	1		0,2080,0416
S236	0,75	3	0,75	0,75	9	0,75		0,755	5		10,1191

Xmax = 10.91

CI= 0.10

CR= 0.068

After дёпёгег the matrix of comparisons and a-cuts between Skyline Web services for the other seven remaining QoS criteria (Q2: *Availability*, Q3: *Throughput*, Q4: *Successfulness*, Q5: *Reliability*, Q6: *Conformance*, Q7: *Good Practice*, Q8: *Latency*), the priority vector and ranking of the K-representative Skyline Web services can be given as follows:

Tableau 36. Skyline Web services priority vectors.

QoS Attributes	Weight	Eigenvectors for each QoS attributes with respect to each Skyline Web service. S447	S1541	S20	S2125	S1736	S1295	S823	S2104	S1371	S236	CR<=0.1
RT	0,28	0,1692	0,0619	0,1570	0,1461	0,0125	0,1363	0,1273	0,0291	0,0416	0,1191	0,068
Avail	0,28	0,0323	0,1464	0,0642	0,1370	0,1284	0,0182	0,1205	0,0168	0,2758	0,0605	0,067
Thr	0,12	0,3110	0,0448	0,0210	0,0193	0,0420	0,0393	0,0912	0,0861	0,1781	0,1672	0,056
Succ	0,12	0,0342	0,1558	0,1453	0,1359	0,1272	0,0127	0,1321	0,0127	0,1220	0,1220	0,073
Relia	0,20	0,0986	0,0210	0,0585	0,0928	0,1863	0,0769	0,0398	0,3233	0,0829	0,0199	0,080
Complia	0,04	0,0878	0,2848	0,0216	0,2639	0,0828	0,0781	0,0200	0,0184	0,0735	0,0692	0,052
Best P	0,12	0,2134	0,0429	0,0402	0,0955	0,1978	0,0899	0,0376	0,1844	0,0845	0,0138	0,054
Latency	0,12	0,0693	0,1777	0,1649	0,0129	0,0625	0,0202	0,1536	0,0612	0,1434	0,1342	0,048
Ifuzzy AHP Score		0,1550	0,1245	0,1191	0,1400	0,1316	0,0812	0,1279	0,1196	0,1718	0,1095	
Rank		2nd	6th	8th	3rd	4th	10th	5th	7th	1st	9th	

6.3.6 Storing Skyline K-representatives Web Services

After calculating the weights of the QoS criteria and the priority vectors of the Skyline web services, the IFAHP score (expression 5.3) is used to rank the k-representative Skyline web services.

Tableau 37. Storage of Skyline k-representative web services.

Rank	1st	2nd	3rd	4th	5th	6th	7th	8th	9th	10th
Service	S1371	S447	S2125	S1736	S823	S1541	S2104	S20	S236	S1295

6.4 Discussion

From the experiments carried out on the two approaches SkyAP-S3 and SEFAP, we can see that its performance depends on the performance of the PROMETHEE method, which is improved by reducing the number of Web services to be taken into account during the ranking phase. Skyline makes it possible to eliminate all domino Web services and focus on the best Web services, however, Skyline is more effective with corrOlO and indOpendant databases than anti-corrOlO databases [Borzsonyi et al., 2001].

The weighting of QoS criteria using AHP, Fuzzy AHP and Entropy allows weights to be assigned to QoS criteria. AHP is frequently used to weight criteria because of its simplicity and its ability to check the consistency of user judgements. The combination of Fuzzy AHP with Entropy has made it possible to take into account the uncertainty in the user's opinion and to exploit the QoS data to calculate the weights.

Comparing the ranking result of the SEFAP approach with existing approaches using the DCG indicator showed that the latter obtains better values; also, the DCG indicator obtained for SEFAP becomes higher when the number of Skyline objects becomes greater.

For the IFAHP approach, it is more efficient for anti-corrOlO and indOpendant databases, it allows to control the size of the result returned by Skyline, using the K-reprOsentative Skyline variant, this approach is very interesting, because, it returns a list of the most relevant Web services, which represents a summary of the entire Skyline output, however, the choice of the value of K in the K-average method represents a determining factor in the number of Skyline Web services returned by the IFAHP approach.

The new version of the Fuzzy AHP method exploits a discretization algorithm to manage the different comparison matrices between Skyline Web Services. This version facilitates the process of weighting the QoS criteria and ranking the Skyline Web Services by requiring less effort from the user on the one hand, and on the other, it exploits the advantages of the Fuzzy AHP method, particularly in the User Preference Olicitation phase. However, changing the number of intervals defined during the QoS data discrOtisation phase can change the list of Skyline Web Services returned.

6.5 Conclusion

In this chapter we have described the various experiments carried out to validate the approaches proposed in our research. To do this, we have developed a prototype that supports several functionalities.

We foundë that using the Skyline mëthode reduced the search space considërablement focusing on relevant Web services that are not dominated by any other service.

For the SkyAP-S3 approach, the use of the AHP method enabled QoS criteria to be weighed in a simple and intuitive way based on the user's opinion. The PROMETHEE method performed partial and total ranking of Skyline Web services, taking into account the user's preferences (criterion weights, preference thresholds, indifference thresholds and preference directions). The performance of the PROMETHEE method was considerably improved by applying it to a reduced set of Skyline Web services.

For the SEFAP approach, the two methods Fuzzy AHP and Entropy were used to weight the QoS criteria taking into account the uncertainty in the users' opinion; the comparison of the ranking result with the existing approaches using the DCG indicator showed that the latter obtains better values; also, the DCG indicator obtained for SEFAP becomes higher when the number of Skyline objects becomes greater.

For the last approach, the K-representative Skyline operator was used to control the volume of Skyline output returning a summary of all Skyline output; We also found that the process of weighting the QoS criteria and ordering the Skyline representative Web services required less effort from the user, for eight QoS criteria, the user is asked to express their priorities on the level of importance of each criterion using linguistic terms, and as a result, the weights are calculated directly in a simple and intuitive way. With the classic Fuzzy AHP method, the user is required to fill in a comparison matrix made up of several entries, which is very difficult in practice, particularly in the field of Web service selection. Therefore, the ranking of Skyline representatives web services was based on QoS data using a discretisation algorithm.

7 General conclusion and outlook

7.1 General conclusion

Web services are software components that enable interoperability between information systems. The standards for describing and publishing services aim to give service consumers all the information they need to interact properly. However, the information offered by

suppliers is information that concerns the functional aspects of services, such as inputs and outputs, and the operations offered. In many cases, therefore, the user searches for services on the basis of other non-functional information, such as response time.
The number of services published by service providers is increasing exponentially. Most of these web services appear with similar functionalities. Choosing the best of these services is a very difficult task for users. The quality of services, QoS, is a decisive criterion in the choice process.
To select a service from a number of candidate services, which offer the same functionality but with different quality of service (QoS), the user cannot test all the candidate services, but can rely on the history of previous invocations by other users. In recent years, Skyline has emerged as a new and popular paradigm for finding the most relevant Web services based on QoS data. This is a promising direction that reduces the user's decision space by offering only those services that are not dominated; however, Skyline has a few drawbacks: i) it returns incomparable results, where the user finds it difficult to express his preferences and choose the relevant services with a better compromise between the criteria, ii) Skyline gives the same importance to all the selection criteria, whereas this importance differs from one context to another and from one domain to another, For example, in e-payment services the *security* criterion is more important than *response time*, iii) the size of the Skyline result cannot be controlled, in fact Skyline can return a very large number of services, which makes the selection process very cumbersome.
In this thesis, we have proposed several solutions to this problem: the first, called SkyAP-S3, is based on the combination of several multi-criteria decision support methods (MCDMs), namely Skyline, AHP and PROMETHEE: Skyline, AHP and PROMETHEE.
We use the Skyline method to reduce the search space to the user. Then, we compute the weights of the QoS criteria based on the AHP method which offers the possibility for users to express their preferences in the form of a binary comparison between each two criteria in a simple and intuitive way, minimising user effort and ensuring that the weights assigned to the criteria are consistent. In the last step, we propose to use the PROMETHEE method to perform a ranking of Skyline Web services, proposing to the user the services that have a good compromise between the QoS criteria, exploiting the outranking relationships and relying on the different functions for expressing preferences on the criteria such as preference indicators, indifference indicators, direction of preferences and criterion weights.
The second proposal, called SEFAP, is an improved version of SkyAP-S3. It involves dealing with uncertainty in user judgements when weighting QoS criteria, using the objective "Entropy" method based on data and the subjective "Fuzzy AHP" method based on user judgement.
In the third approach, we propose an improved version of the Fuzzy AHP method for ranking Skyline Web services, such that the comparison matrices between QoS criteria and between representative Skyline Web services will be generated automatically by exploiting a discretisation algorithm on the QoS data.
To demonstrate the effectiveness of these approaches, we have developed a prototype that implements the computation of Skyline requests and enables a ranking of Skyline Web services to be established, taking into account user preferences and the weights of QoS criteria. The experiments are carried out on real QoS data, and we have carried out comparative studies with existing approaches. The results show that our approaches select the most relevant Web services to meet the user's preferences.

7.2 Outlook

The approaches outlined in this thesis can be extended in several directions:

- Reducing the number of QoS criteria to be considered in the Web services selection process can significantly improve the effectiveness of the Skyline method, by focusing only on the most relevant QoS criteria;
- Parallel implementation of the proposed algorithms, using parallel computing frameworks such as MapReduce, can improve the approaches proposed in this work, thanks to the distribution of QoS data and the distribution of processing (Skyline computing algorithms and Skyline Web services ordering algorithms);
- In turn, the multi-body architecture represents a very interesting technology that can be exploited to reduce the computation time of Skyline requests by adapting existing sequential algorithms so that they can be executed in parallel;
- Extension of the proposed approaches to enable better composition of Skyline Web services; the principle is to study the possibility of integrating the proposed approaches as a brick in the composition process and make comparisons with similar work;
- With the rapid development of cloud computing in recent years, adapting the work proposed in this thesis to meet the requirements of cloud computing environments is a promising direction, with implementation on cloud simulators.

List of publications

- **International review :**

Ouadah, A., Hadjali, A., Nader, F., et al. (2018). "SEFAP: an efficient approach for ranking Skyline Web services". Journal of Ambient Intelligence & Humanized Computing (2018). https://doi.org/10.1007/s12652-018-0721-7, (**Ranked Q1, IF 2017 = 1.588**), Journal indexed by SCOPUS and Clarivate Analytics (Thomson Reuters).

- **International conferences :**

Ouadah, A., Benouaret, K., Hadjali, A., & Nader, F. (2015, April). Combining skyline and multi-criteria decision methods to enhance Web services selection. In *Programming and Systems (ISPS), 2015 12th International Symposium on* (pp. 1-8). IEEE. Doi: 10.1109/ISPS.2015.7244975 ;

Ouadah, A., Benouaret, K., Hadjali, A., & Nader, F. (2015, October). Skyap-s3: A hybrid approach for efficient skyline services selection. In *Service-Oriented Computing and Applications (SOCA), 2015 IEEE 8th International Conference on* (pp. 18-25). IEEE.. doi: 10.1109/SOCA.2015.22 (**Core C**);

Ouadah, A., Hadjali, A., Nader, F., (2018, June). A QoS History Record-based Framework for K-Representative Skyline Web Services Selection. In *IEEE International Conference on Web Services (ICWS), 2018*. (**Core A**).

Ouadah A., Hadjali A., Nader F. (2018, October). A Hybrid MCDM Framework for Efficient Web Services Selection Based on QoS. *International Conference on Applied Smart Systems* (ICASS'2018). IEEE, 24-25November 2018, Mëdëa, Algeria. 10.1109/ICASS.2018.8652037

Ouadah, A., Hadjali, A., Nader, F., & Benouaret, K. (2018, December). An Improved Fuzzy Analytical Hierarchy Process for K-Representative Skyline Web Services Selection. In *International Symposium on Modelling and Implementation of Complex Systems* (pp. 312-328). Springer, Cham. Doi: 10.1007/978-3-030-05481-6 24

Bibliography

[Al-Masri et al. 2007a] Al-Masri, E., & Mahmoud, Q. H. (2007, August). Qos-based discovery and ranking of web services. *In Computer Communications and Networks, 2007. ICCCN 2007. Proceedings of 16th International Conference on* (pp. 529-534). IEEE.

[Al-Masri et al., 2007b] Al-Masri, E., & Mahmoud, Q. H. (2009, October). Discovering the best web service: A neural network-based solution. *In Systems, Man and Cybernetics, 2009. SMC 2009. IEEE International Conference on* (pp. 4250-4255). IEEE.

[Al-Masri et al., 2007c] Al-Masri, E., & Mahmoud, Q. H. (2007, May). Crawling multiple UDDI business registries. *In Proceedings of the 16th international conference on World Wide Web* (pp. 1255-1256). ACM.

[Alam et al., 2016] Alam, K. A., & Ahmad, R. (2016). A hybrid fuzzy multi-criteria decision model for cloud service selection and importance degree of component services in service compositions. In *Uncertainty Modelling in Knowledge Engineering and Decision Making: Proceedings of the 12 th International FLINS Conference*(pp. 334-340).

[Albadvi et al., 2007] Albadvi, A., Chaharsooghi, S. K., & Esfahanipour, A. (2007). Decision making in stock trading: An application of PROMETHEE. *European Journal of Operational Research, 177*(2), 673-683.

[Almulla et al., 2011] Almulla, M., Almatori, K., & Yahyaoui, H. (2011, July). A qos-based fuzzy model for ranking real world web services. *In Web Services (ICWS), 2011 IEEE International Conference on* (pp. 203-210). IEEE.

[Almulla et al., 2015] Almulla M, Yahyaoui H, Al-Matori K (2015) A new fuzzy hybrid technique for ranking real world Web services. *KnowlBased Syst* 77:1-15.

[Alrifai et al., 2009] Alrifai, M., & Risse, T. (2009, April). Combining global optimization with local selection for efficient QoS-aware service composition. In *Proceedings of the 18th international conference on World wide Web* (pp. 881-890). ACM.

[Alrifai et al., 2010] Alrifai, M., Skoutas, D., & Risse, T. (2010, April). Selecting Skyline services for QoS-based Web service composition. *In Proceedings of the 19th international conference on World Wide Web* (pp. 11-20). ACM.

[Arsanjani 2004] Arsanjani, A. (2004). Service-oriented modeling and architecture. *IBM developer works*, 1, 15.

[Ayadi 2010] Ayadi, D. (2010). Optimisation multicritere de la fiabilit^: application du modele de goal programming avec les fonctions de satisfactions dans l'industrie de traitement de gaz (Doctoral dissertation, Universite d'Angers).

[Balali et al., 2014] Balali, V., Zahraie, B., & Roozbahani, A. (2014). A comparison of AHP and PROMETHEE family decision making methods for selection of building structural system. *American Journal of Civil Engineering and Architecture*, 2(5), 149-159.

[Barrios et al., 2016] Barrios, M. A. O., De Felice, F., Negrete, K. P., Romero, B. A., Arenas, A. Y., & Petrillo, A. (2016). An AHP-Topsis Integrated Model for Selecting the Most Appropriate Tomography Equipment. *International Journal of Information Technology & Decision Making*, 15(04), 861-885.

[Beckmann et al., 1990] Beckmann, N., Kriegel, H. P., Schneider, R., & Seeger, B. (1990, May). The R*-tree: an efficient and robust access method for points and rectangles. In *Acm Sigmod Record*(Vol. 19, No. 2, pp. 322-331). Acm.

[Behzadian et al., 2010] Behzadian, M., Kazemzadeh, R. B., Albadvi, A., & Aghdasi, M. (2010). PROMETHEE: A comprehensive literature review on methodologies and applications. *European journal of Operational research*, *200*(1), 198-215.

[Bellwood et al., 2002] Bellwood, T., Cement, L., Ehnebuske, D., Hately, A., Hondo, M., Husband, Y. L., ... & von Riegen, C. (2002). UDDI Version 3.0. *Published specification, Oasis*, *5*, 16-18.

[Ben Halima 2009] Riadh BEN HALIMA. "Design, implementation and experimentation of a bus architecture for Tauto-repair of service-based distributed applications" . 2009. These de doctorat. Universite Toulouse III - Paul Sabatier et la Faculte des Sciences Economiques et de Gestion - Sfax.

[Benouaret et al., 2011] Benouaret, K., Benslimane, D., & Hadjali, A. (2011, July). On the use of fuzzy dominance for computing service skyline based on qos. In *2011 IEEE International Conference on Web Services*(pp. 540-547). IEEE.

[Benouaret 2012] Benouaret, K. (2012). *Advanced techniques for web service query optimization* (Doctoral dissertation, Universite Claude Bernard-Lyon I).

[Benouaret et al., 2012a] Benouaret, K., Benslimane, D., & Hadjali, A. (2012, June). Ws-sky: An efficient and flexible framework for qos-aware web service selection. In *Services Computing (SCC), 2012 IEEE Ninth International Conference on* (pp. 146-153). IEEE.

[Benouaret et al., 2012b] Benouaret, K., Benslimane, D., & Hadjali, A. (2012, June). Selecting skyline web services for multiple users preferences. In *Web Services (ICWS), 2012 IEEE 19th International Conference on* (pp. 635-636). IEEE.

[Benouaret et al., 2012c] Benouaret, K., Sacharidis, D., Benslimane, D., & Hadjali, A. (2012, November). Majority-Rule-Based Web service selection. In *International Conference on Web Information Systems Engineering* (pp. 689-695). Springer, Berlin, Heidelberg.

[Benouaret et al., 2012d] Benouaret, K., Benslimane, D., & Hadjali, A. (2012, June). Selecting skyline Web services from uncertain qos. In *Services Computing (SCC), 2012 IEEE Ninth International Conference on* (pp. 523-530). IEEE.

[Booth et al., 2004] Booth, D. Haas, H. McCabe, F. Newcomer, E. Champion, M. Ferris, C. Orchard, D. (2004). W3C Web Service Architecture Group, Web Services Architecture. : W3C- WSA-Group, http://www.w3.org/TR/ws-arch.

[Bouanaka et al., 2013] Bouanaka, M. A., & Zarour, N. (2013). An approach for an optimized Web service selection based on skyline.*International Journal of Computer Science Issues (IJCSI)*, *10* (1), 412.

[Brans et al., 1986] Brans, J. P., Vincke, P., & Mareschal, B. (1986). How to select and how to rank projects: The PROMETHEE method. *European journal of operational research*, 24(2), 228-238.

[Brans et al., 1994] Brans, J. P., & Mareschal, B. (1994). The PROMCALC & GAIA decision support system for multicriteria decision aid. *Decision support systems*, *12*(4-5), 297-310.

[Brans et al., 2005] Brans, J. P., & Mareschal, B. (2005). PROMETHEE methods. *InMultiple criteria decision analysis: state of the art surveys* (pp. 163-186). Springer, New York, NY.

[Bray et al., 2006] Bray, T., Paoli, J., Sperberg-McQueen, C. M., Maler, E., & Yergeau, F. (1997). Extensible markup language (XML). *World Wide Web Journal*, *2*(4), 27-66. http://www.w3.org/TR/xml11.

[Borzsonyi et al., 2001] Borzsony, S., Kossmann, D., & Stocker, K. (2001). The skyline operator. In *Data Engineering, 2001. Proceedings. 17th International Conference on* (pp. 421430). IEEE.

[Box et al., 2000] Box, D., Ehnebuske, D., Kakivaya, G., Layman, A., Mendelsohn, N., Nielsen, H. F., ... & Winer, D. (2000). Simple object access protocol (SOAP) 1.1.

[Buyukozkan et al., 2012] Buyukozkan, G., & Qifgi, G. (2012). A combined fuzzy AHP and fuzzy TOPSIS based strategic analysis of electronic service quality in healthcare industry. *Expert Systems with Applications*,39(3), 2341-2354.

[Buckley 1985] Buckley JJ (1985) Fuzzy hierarchical analysis. *Fuzzy Sets Syst* 17(3):233-247.

[Chakhar et al., 2011] Chakhar, S., Youcef, S., Mousseau, V., Mokdad, L., & Haddad, S. (2011). Multicriteria evaluation-based conceptual framework for composite Web service selection. *Lamsade, University Paris Dauphine, France, Research Report.*

[Chan et al., 2006] Chan, C. Y., Jagadish, H. V., Tan, K. L., Tung, A. K., & Zhang, Z. (2006, June). Finding k-dominant skylines in high dimensional space. In *Proceedings of the 2006ACM SIGMOD international conference on Management of data* (pp. 503-514). ACM.

[Chan et al., 2006] Chan, C. Y., Jagadish, H. V., Tan, K. L., Tung, A. K., & Zhang, Z. (2006, March). On high dimensional skylines. In *International Conference on Extending Database Technology* (pp. 478-495). Springer, Berlin, Heidelberg.

[Chang 1996] Chang, D. Y. (1996). Applications of the extent analysis method on fuzzy AHP. *European Journal of Operation Research*, 95, 649-655.

[Chen et al., 2010] Chen, L., Wu, J., Deng, S., & Li, Y. (2010, July). Service recommendation: Similarity-based representative skyline. *InServices (SERVICES-1), 2010 6th World Congress on* (pp. 360-366). IEEE.

[Christensen et al., 2001] Christensen, E., Curbera, F., Meredith, G., & Weerawarana, S. (2001).

Web services description language (WSDL) 1.1.W3C, http://www.w3.org/TR/wsdl.

[Curbera et al., 2002] Curbera, F., Duftler, M., Khalaf, R., Nagy, W., Mukhi, N., & Weerawarana, S. (2002). Unraveling the Web services web: an introduction to SOAP, WSDL, and UDDI. *IEEE Internet computing*, *6*(2), 86-93.

[Dai et al., 2013] Dai, G., & Qingsheng, Z. (2013). Using skyline and dominance relationship for web ranking services. *Newspaper of Computational Information Systems*, *9*(10), 39773984.

[Dougherty et al., 1995] Dougherty, J., Kohavi, R., & Sahami, M. (1995, July). Supervised and unsupervised discretization of continuous features. In *Machine learning: proceedings of the twelfth international conference* (Vol. 12, pp. 194-202).

[Ennaceur 2015] Ennaceur, A. (2015). *New AHP methods for handling uncertainty within the Belief Function Theory* (Doctoral dissertation, Artois).

[Erl 2004] Erl, T. (2004). Service-oriented architecture: a field guide to integrating XML and Web services. Prentice hall.

[Feder et al., 1988] Feder, T., & Greene, D. (1988, January). Optimal algorithms for approximate clustering. In *Proceedings of the twentieth annual ACM symposium on Theory of computing* (pp. 434-444). ACM.

[Fielding et al., 2000] Fielding, R. T., & Taylor, R. N. (2000). *Architectural styles and the design of network-based software architectures* (Vol. 7). Doctoral dissertation: University of California, Irvine.

[Flajolet et al., 1985] Flajolet, P., & Martin, G. N. (1985). Probabilistic counting algorithms for data base applications. *Journal of computer and system sciences*, *31*(2), 182-209.

[Garcia et al., 2013] Garcia, S., Luengo, J., Saez, J. A., Lopez, V., & Herrera, F. (2013). A survey of discretization techniques: Taxonomy and empirical analysis in supervised learning. *IEEE Transactions on Knowledge and Data Engineering,* 25(4), 734-750.

[Godse et al., 2008] Godse M, Sonar R, Mulik S (2008) The analytical hierarchy process approach for prioritizing features in the selection of Web service. In: Web services. ECOWS'08. IEEE sixth European conference, IEEE, pp 41-50.

[Goldberg 1988] Goldberg, D. E., & Holland, J. H. (1988). Genetic algorithms and machine learning. Machine learning, 3(2), 95-99.

[Gottschalk 2000] Gottschalk, K. (2000) Web Services architecture overview. *IBM whitepaper, IBM developerWorks, 1.*

[Gwyduk et al., 2006] Yeom, G., Yun, T., & Min, D. (2006, April). A QoS model and testing mechanism for quality-driven web services selection. In *Software Technologies for Future Embedded and Ubiquitous Systems, 2006 and the 2006 Second International Workshop on Collaborative Computing, Integration, and Assurance. SEUS 2006/WCCIA 2006. The Fourth IEEE Workshop on* (pp. 6-pp). IEEE.

[Gudgin et al 2003] Gudgin, M., Hadley, M., Mendelsohn, N., Moreau, J. J., Nielsen, H. F., Karmarkar, A., & Lafon, Y. (2003). Simple object access protocol (SOAP) 1.2. *World Wide Web Consortium.*

[Halfaoui 2017] Halfaoui bpouse Ghernaout, A. (2017). *La sélection des services Web dans une composition a base de criteres non fonctionnels* (Doctoral dissertation, 19/03/2017), Universitb de Tlemcen.

[Halfaoui et al., 2015] Halfaoui, A., Hadjila, F., & Didi, F. (2015, May). Qos-aware Web services selection based on fuzzy dominance. In *IFIP International Conference on Computer Science and its Applications_x000D_* (pp. 291-300) Springer, Cham.

[He et al., 2017] He, Q., Zhou, R., Zhang, X., Wang, Y., Ye, D., Chen, F., ... & Yang, Y. (2017). Keyword search for building service-based systems. *IEEE Transactions on Software Engineering,* 43(7), 658-674.

[Herssens et al., 2008] Herssens, C., Jureta, I. J., & Faulkner, S. (2008, June). Dealing with quality tradeoffs during service selection. In *2008 International Conference on Autonomic Computing* (pp. 77-86). IEEE.

[Hjaltason et al., 1999] Hjaltason, G. R., & Samet, H. (1999). Distance browsing in spatial databases. *ACM Transactions on Database Systems (TODS)*, *24*(2), 265-318.

[Hyde et al., 2003] Hyde, K., Maier, H. R., & Colby, C. (2003). Incorporating uncertainty in the PROMETHEE MCDA method. *Journal of Multi-Criteria Decision Analysis*, 12(4-5), 245259.

[Hwang et al., 1981] Hwang, C. L., & Yoon, K. (1981). Methods for multiple attribute decision making. In *Multiple attribute decision making* (pp. 58-191). Springer, Berlin, Heidelberg.

[Jain 2010] Jain, A. K. (2010). Data clustering: 50 years beyond K-means. *Pattern recognition letters*, 31(8).

[Jarvelin et al., 2012] Jarvelin, K., & Kekalainen, J. (2002). Cumulated gain-based evaluation of IR techniques. *ACM Transactions on Information Systems* (TOIS), 20(4), 422-446.

[Kangas et al., 2001] Kangas, A., Kangas, J., & Pykalainen, J. (2001). Outranking methods as tools in strategic natural resources planning.

[Karim et al., 2011] Karim, R., Ding, C., & Chi, C. H. (2011, July). An enhanced PROMETHEE model for QoS-based Web service selection. In *Services Computing (SCC), 2011 IEEE International Conference on* (pp. 536-543). IEEE.

[Kangchan et al., 2003] Lee, K., Jeon, J., Lee, W., Jeong, S. H., & Park, S. W. (2003). Qos for web services: Requirements and possible approaches. *W3C working group note*, *25*(3), 1-9.

[Kaya et al., 2011] Kaya, T., & Kahraman, C. (2011). A fuzzy approach to e-banking Website quality assessment based on an integrated AHP-ELECTRE method. *Technological and Economic Development of Economy*, 17(2), 313-334

[Kritikos et al., 2009] Kritikos, K., & Plexousakis, D. (2009). Mixed-integer programming for QoS-based web service matchmaking. *IEEE Transactions on Services Computing*, *2*(2), 122139.

[Kossmann et al., 2002] Kossmann, D., Ramsak, F., & Rost, S. (2002, August). Shooting stars in the sky: An online algorithm for skyline queries. In *Proceedings of the 28th international conference on Very Large Data Bases* (pp. 275-286). VLDB Endowment.

[Kumar et al., 2016] Kumar, S., & Purohit, L. (2016, December). Exploring k-means clustering and skyline for Web service selection. *InIndustrial and Information Systems (ICIIS), 2016 11th International Conference on* (pp. 603-607). IEEE.

[Kumar et al., 2017] Kumar, R. R., Mishra, S., & Kumar, C. (2017). Prioritizing the solution of cloud service selection using integrated MCDM methods under Fuzzy environment. *The Journal of Supercomputing*, *73*(11), 4652-4682.

[Kumar et al., 2018] Kumar, R. R., & Kumar, C. (2018). A Multi Criteria Decision Making Method for Cloud Service Selection and Ranking.*International Journal of Ambient Computing and Intelligence (IJACI)*, *9* (3), 1-14.

[Kung et al., 1975] Kung, H. T., Luccio, F., & Preparata, F. P. (1975). On finding the maxima of a set of vectors. *Journal of the ACM (JACM)*, *22*(4), 469-476.

[Kwong et al., 2002] Kwong, C. K., & Bai, H. (2002). A fuzzy AHP approach to the determination of importance weights of customer requirements in quality function deployment. *Journal of intelligent manufacturing*, 13(5), 367-377.

[Lahby 2013] Lahby, M. (2013). *Optimisation et évaluation des performances des communications mobiles dans un environnement reseaux multi-acces* (Doctoral dissertation, Universite Hassan II Mohammedia-Casablanca).

[Laarhoven et al., 1983] Laarhoven Van PJM, Pedrycz W (1983) A fuzzy extension of Saaty's priority theory. *Fuzzy Sets Syst* 11(1-3):229-241.

[Legner 2007] Legner, C. (2007, September). Is there a market for web services? In *International Conference on Service-Oriented Computing* (pp. 29-42). Springer, Berlin, Heidelberg.

[Lin et al., 2007] Lin, X., Yuan, Y., Zhang, Q., & Zhang, Y. (2007, April). Selecting stars: The k most representative skyline operator. In *Data Engineering, 2007. ICDE 2007. IEEE 23rd International Conference on* (pp. 86-95). IEEE. doi:10.1109/ICDE.2007.367854

[Lin et al., 2016] Lin, C. L., Shih, Y. H., Tzeng, G. H., & Yu, H. C. (2016). A service selection model for digital music service platforms using a hybrid MCDM approach. *Applied Soft Computing*, *48*, 385-403.

[Liu et al., 2017] Liu, F., Peng, Y., Zhang, W., & Pedrycz, W. (2017). On Consistency in AHP and Fuzzy AHP. *Journal of Systems Science and Information*, *5*(2), 128-147.

[Lopez-velasco 2008] Lopez-Velasco, C. (2008). *Selection and composition of Web services for the generation of context-aware applications* (Doctoral dissertation, Universite Joseph-Fourier-Grenoble I).

[Ma et al., 2013] Ma, Y., Wang, S., Sun, Q., Zou, H., & Yang, F. (2013, June). Web services qos measure based on subjective and objective weight. In *Services Computing (SCC), 2013 IEEE International Conference on* (pp. 543-550). IEEE.

[Macharis et al., 2004] Macharis, C., Springael, J., De Brucker, K., & Verbeke, A. (2004). PROMETHEE and AHP: The design of operational synergies in multicriteria analysis:

Strengthening PROMETHEE with ideas of AHP. *European Journal of Operational Research*, 153(2), 307-317

[MacKenzie et al., 2006] MacKenzie, C. M., Laskey, K., McCabe, F., Brown, P. F., Metz, R., & Hamilton, B. A. (2006). Reference model for service oriented architecture 1.0. *OASIS standard*, 12, 18.

[Mani et al., 2002] Mani, A., & Nagarajan, A. (2005). Understanding quality of service for Web services. *IBM developerWorks*.

[Marin 2008] Marin, C. (2008). *Une approche orientee domaine pour la composition de services* (Doctoral dissertation, Grenoble 1).

[Marinoni 2006] Marinoni, O. (2006). A discussion on the computational limitations of outranking methods for land-use suitability assessment. *International Journal of Geographical Information Science*, 20(1), 69-87.

[McLain el al., 1974] McLain, D. H. (1974). Drawing contours from arbitrary data points. *The Computer Journal*, *17*(4), 318-324.

[Mitra et al,. 2007] Mitra, N., & Lafon, Y. (2003). Soap version 1.2 part 0: Primer.*W3C recommendation*, *24*, 12.

[Mohammadshahi et al., 2013] Mohammadshahi, Y. (2013). A state-of-art survey on TQM applications using MCDM techniques. *Decision Science Letters*, *2*(3), 125-134.

[Nacer et al., 2015] Nacer, A. A., Bessai, K., Youcef, S., & Godart, C. (2015, June). A multicriteria based approach for Web service selection using quality of service (qos). In *Services Computing (SCC), 2015 IEEE International Conference on* (pp. 570-577). IEEE.

[Nefeslioglu et al., 2013] Nefeslioglu, H. A., Sezer, E. A., Gokceoglu, C., & Ayas, Z. (2013). A modified analytical hierarchy process (M-AHP) approach for decision support systems in natural hazard assessments.*Computers & Geosciences,* 59, 1-8.

[Onut et al., 2008] Onut, S., Kara, S. S., & Efendigil, T. (2008). A hybrid fuzzy MCDM approach to machine tool selection. *Journal of intelligent manufacturing*, 19(4), 443-453.

[Ouadah et al., 2015a] Ouadah, A., Benouaret, K., Hadjali, A., & Nader, F. (2015, April). Combining skyline and multi-criteria decision methods to enhance Web services selection. In *Programming and Systems (ISPS), 2015 12th International Symposium on* (pp. 1-8). IEEE.

[Ouadah et al., 2015b] Ouadah, A., Benouaret, K., Hadjali, A., & Nader, F. (2015, October). Skyap-s3: A hybrid approach for efficient skyline services selection. In *Service-Oriented Computing and Applications (SOCA), 2015 IEEE 8th International Conference on* (pp. 18-25). IEEE.

[Ouadah et al., 2018a] Ouadah, A., Hadjali, A., Nader, F. et al. (2018). SEFAP: an efficient approach for ranking Skyline Web services. *J Ambient Intell Human Comput* (2018).

[Ouadah et al., 2018b] Ouadah, A., Hadjali, A., Nader, F., (2018, June). A QoS History Recordbased Framework for K-Representative Skyline Web Services Selection. In *IEEE International Conference on Web Services (ICWS), 2018.*

[Ouadah et al., 2018c] Ouadah A., Hadjali A., Nader F. (2018) "A Hybrid MCDM Framework for Efficient Web Services Selection Based on QoS", *International Conference on Applied Smart Systems* (ICASS'2018). IEEE, 24-25 November 2018, Mëdëa, Algeria.

[Ouadah et al., 2018d] Ouadah, A., Hadjali, A., Nader, F., & Benouaret, K. (2018, December). An Improved Fuzzy Analytical Hierarchy Process for K-Representative Skyline Web Services Selection. In *International Symposium on Modelling and Implementation of Complex Systems* (pp. 312-328). Springer, Cham.

[Papadias et al., 2003] Papadias, D., Tao, Y., Fu, G., & Seeger, B. (2003, June). An optimal and progressive algorithm for skyline queries. *InProceedings of the 2003 ACM SIGMOD international conference on Management of data* (pp. 467-478). ACM.

[Papadias et al., 2005] Papadias, D., Tao, Y., Fu, G., & Seeger, B. (2005). Progressive skyline computation in database systems. *ACM Transactions on Database Systems (TODS)*, *30*(1), 4182.

[Papazoglou 2003] Papazoglou, M. P. (2003, December). Service-oriented computing: Concepts, characteristics and directions. In *Web Information Systems Engineering*, 2003. WISE 2003. Proceedings of the Fourth International Conference on (pp. 3-12). IEEE.

[Papazoglou el al., 2004] Papazoglou, M. P., & Dubray, J. J. (2004). *A survey of web service technologies*. University of Trento.

[Papazoglou el al., 2007] Papazoglou, M. P., & Van Den Heuvel, W. J. (2007). Service oriented architectures: approaches, technologies and research issues. *The VLDB journal*, 16(3), 389-415.

[Peng et al., 2013] Peng, A. H., & Xiao, X. M. (2013). Material selection using PROMETHEE combined with analytic network process under hybrid environment. *Materials & Design*, *47*, 643-652.

[Preparata et al., 1985] Preparata, F. P., & Shamos, M. I. (1985). *Computational geometry: an introduction*. Springer Science & Business Media.

[Ran 2003] Ran, S. (2003). A model for web services discovery with QoS.*ACM Sigecom exchanges*, *4* (1), 1-10.

[Rehman et al., 2012] Rehman ur, Z., Hussain, O. K., & Hussain, F. K. (2012, September). Iaas cloud selection using MCDM methods. In *2012 IEEE Ninth international conference on ebusiness engineering*(pp. 246-251). IEEE.

[Rehman et al., 2014] Rehman urZ, Hussain OK, Hussain FK (2014). Parallel cloud service selection and ranking based on QoS history. *Int J Parallel Prog* 42(5):820-852

[Robertson et al., 1999] Robertson, S., & Robertson, J. (2012). *Mastering the requirements process: Getting requirements right*. Addison-wesley.

[Roy 1968] Roy, B. (1968). Classification and choice in the presence of multiple points of view. *Revue franjaise d'informatique et de recherche operationnelle*, *2*(8), 57-75.

[Roy at al., 2003] Roy, B., Figueira, J. R., & Almeida-Dias, J. (2014). Discriminating thresholds as a tool to cope with imperfect knowledge in multiple criteria decision aiding: theoretical results and practical issues. *Omega*, *43*, 9-20.

[Saaty 1987] Saaty, R. W. (1987). The analytic hierarchy process-what it is and how it is used. *Mathematical modelling*, *9*(3-5), 161-176.

[Saaty 1996] Saaty, T. (1996). Decision making with dependence and feedback: The analytic network process. *RWS Publications*.

[Serrai et al., 2016] Serrai W, Abdelli A, Mokdad L, Hammal Y (2016). An efficient approach for Web service selection. *Comput Commun (ISCC), 2016 IEEE symposium*, IEEE, pp 167172.

[Serrai et al., 2017] Serrai, W., Abdelli, A., Mokdad, L., & Hammal, Y. (2017). Towards an efficient and a more accurate web service selection using MCDM methods. *Journal of computational science*, *22*, 253-267.

[Seo et al., 2004] Seo, Y. J., Jeong, H. Y., & Song, Y. J. (2004, December). A study on Web services selection method based on the negotiation through quality broker: A maut-based approach. In *International Conference on Embedded Software and Systems* (pp. 65-73). Springer, Berlin, Heidelberg.

[Seo et al., 2005] Seo, Y. J., Jeong, H. Y., & Song, Y. J. (2005, December). Best web service selection based on the decision making between QoS criteria of service. In *International Conference on Embedded Software and Systems* (pp. 408-419). Springer, Berlin, Heidelberg.

[Shannon 1948] Shannon, C. E. (1948). A mathematical theory of communication. *Bell system technical journal*, *27*(3), 379-423.

[Shao et al., 2007] Shao, L., Zhang, J., Wei, Y., Zhao, J., Xie, B., & Mei, H. (2007, July). Personalized qos prediction forweb services via collaborative filtering. In *Web Services, 2007. ICWS 2007. IEEE International Conference on* (pp. 439-446). IEEE.

[Silas et al., 2012] Silas, S., Rajsingh, E. B., & Ezra, K. (2012). Efficient service selection middleware using ELECTRE methodology for cloud environments. *Information Technology Journal*, *11*(7), 868.

[Skoutas et al., 2010] Skoutas, D., Sacharidis, D., Simitsis, A., & Sellis, T. (2010). Ranking and clustering Web services using multicriteria dominance relationships. *IEEE Transactions on Services Computing*, (3), 163-177.

[Sun et al., 2014] Sun L, Dong H, Hussain FK, Hussain OK, Ma J, Zhang Y (2014). A hybrid fuzzy framework for cloud service selection. In: *Web services (ICWS), 2014 IEEE international conference*, IEEE, pp 313-320.

[Sun et al., 2016] Sun, R., Zhang, B., & Liu, T. (2016, May). Ranking web service for high quality by applying improved Entropy-TOPSIS method. In *Software Engineering, Artificial Intelligence, Networking and Parallel/Distributed Computing (SNPD), 2016 17th IEEE/ACIS International Conference on* (pp. 249-254). IEEE.

[Tan et al., 2001] Tan, K. L., Eng, P. K., & Ooi, B. C. (2001, September). Efficient progressive skyline computation. In *VLDB* (Vol. 1, pp. 301-310).

[Tang 2009] Tang, Y. C. (2009). An approach to budget allocation for an aerospace company-Fuzzy analytic hierarchy process and artificial neural network. *Neurocomputing*, *72* (16-18), 3477-3489.

[Tao et al., 2009] Tao, Y., Ding, L., Lin, X., & Pei, J. (2009, March). Distance-based representative Skyline. In Data Engineering, 2009. ICDE'09. IEEE 25th International Conference on (pp. 892-903). IEEE. doi: https://doi.org/10.1109/ICDE.2009.84.

[Thio at al., 2005] Thio, N., & Karunasekera, S. (2005, March). Automatic measurement of a qos metric for web service recommendation. In *Software Engineering Conference, 2005. Proceedings. 2005 Australian* (pp. 202-211). IEEE.

[Tiakas et al., 2007] Tiakas, E., Papadopoulos, A. N., & Manolopoulos, Y. (2007). Top-k Dominating Queries.

[Vlachou et al., 2010] Vlachou, A., & Vazirgiannis, M. (2010). Ranking the sky: Discovering the importance of skyline points through subspace dominance relationships. *Data & Knowledge Engineering*, 69(9), 943-964.

[Vesyropoulos et al., 2015] Vesyropoulos, N., & Georgiadis, C. K. (2015). QoS-Based Filters in Web Service Compositions: Utilizing Multi-Criteria Decision Analysis Methods. *Journal of Multi-Criteria Decision Analysis*, 22(5-6), 279-292.

[Vincke 1992] Vincke, P. (1992). *Multicriteria decision-aid*. John Wiley & Sons.

[Vogel et al., 1995] Vogel, A., Kerherve, B., von Bochmann, G., & Gecsei, J. (1995). Distributed multimedia and QoS: A survey. *IEEE multimedia*,*2*(2), 10-19.

[Wang et al., 2007] Wang, J. J., & Yang, D. L. (2007). Using a hybrid multi-criteria decision aid method for information systems outsourcing. *Computers & Operations Research*, 34(12), 3691-3700.

[Whaiduzzaman at al., 2014] Whaiduzzaman, M., Gani, A., Anuar, N. B., Shiraz, M., Haque, M. N., & Haque, I. T. (2014). Cloud service selection using multicriteria decision analysis. *The Scientific World Journal,2014.*

[Wang et al., 2008] Wang, T. C., & Chen, Y. H. (2008). Applying fuzzy linguistic preference relations to the improvement of consistency of fuzzy AHP. *Information Sciences*, 178(19), 3755-3765.

[Weider et al., 2007] Weider, Y. W. D., Radhakrishna, R. B., Pingali, S., & Kolluri, V. (2007). Modeling the measurements of QoS requirements in web service systems. *Simulation, 83* (1), 75-91.

[Weyuker et al., 2002] Weyuker, E. J., & Avritzer, A. (2002). A metric to predict software scalability. In *Software metrics, 2002. proceedings. eighth ieee symposium on* (pp. 152-158). IEEE.

[Xiong et al., 2007] Xiong, P., & Fan, Y. (2007, August). Qos-aware web service selection by a synthetic weight. In *Fuzzy Systems and Knowledge Discovery, 2007. FSKD 2007. Fourth International Conference on* (Vol. 3, pp. 632-637). IEEE.

[Yiu et al., 2007] Yiu, M. L., & Mamoulis, N. (2007, September). Efficient processing of top-k dominating queries on multi-dimensional data. In *Proceedings of the 33rd international conference on Very large data bases* (pp. 483-494). VLDB Endowment.

[Yu et al., 2009] Yu, Q., & Bouguettaya, A. (2009). Foundations for efficient Web service selection. Springer Science & Business Media.

[Yu et al., 2010a] Yu, Q., & Bouguettaya, A. (2010, July). Computing service skylines over sets of services. In *Web Services (ICWS), 2010 IEEE International Conference on* (pp. 481488). IEEE.

[Yu et al., 2010b] Yu, Q., & Bouguettaya, A. (2010). Computing service skyline from uncertain qows. *IEEE Transactions on Services Computing, 3*(1), 16-29.

[Yu et al., 2011] Yu, Q., & Bouguettaya, A. (2013). Efficient service skyline computation for composite service selection. *IEEE Transactions on Knowledge and Data Engineering, 25*(4), 776-789.

[Zadeh 1965] Zadeh L.A. (1965). Fuzzy sets. Information and Control, 8(3), pp. 338-353.

[Zeng et al., 2004] Zeng, L., Benatallah, B., Ngu, A. H., Dumas, M., Kalagnanam, J., & Chang, H. (2004). QoS-aware middleware for web services composition. *IEEE Transactions on software engineering, 30*(5), 311-327.

[Zhang et al., 2018] Zhang, Y. W., Zhou, Y. Y., Wang, F. T., Sun, Z., & He, Q. (2018). Service recommendation based on quotient space granularity analysis and covering algorithm on Spark. *Knowledge-Based Systems, 147*, 25-35.

[Zhu 2014] Zhu, K. (2014). Fuzzy analytic hierarchy process: Fallacy of the popular methods. *European Journal of Operational Research, 236*(1), 209-217.

MIX
Papier aus verantwortungsvollen Quellen
Paper from responsible sources
FSC® C105338

FSC
www.fsc.org

Printed by Books on Demand GmbH, Norderstedt / Germany